REVIVAL,
HALLELUJAH!
FROM THE SHOULDER

PAUL JUBY

Inspiring Voices®
A Service of Guideposts

Inspiring Voices books may be ordered through booksellers or by contacting:

Inspiring Voices
1663 Liberty Drive
Bloomington, IN 47403
www.inspiringvoices.com
1-(866) 697-5313

Because of the dynamic nature of the Internet, any web addresses or links contained in this book may have changed since publication and may no longer be valid. The views expressed in this work are solely those of the author and do not necessarily reflect the views of the publisher, and the publisher hereby disclaims any responsibility for them.

Any people depicted in stock imagery provided by Thinkstock are models, and such images are being used for illustrative purposes only.

Certain stock imagery © Thinkstock.

ISBN: 978-1-4624-0128-4 (sc)
ISBN: 978-1-4624-0127-7 (e)

Library of Congress Control Number: 2012906355

Printed in the United States of America

Inspiring Voices rev. date: 05/15/2012

FOREWORD

Out of the blue, I started writing poems. Not beautiful ones, not pretty ones, but all with solid messages of hope and direction. These are messages from the shoulder to church leaders and passive Christians and poems to show the way to all seekers. These poems can be read to congregations to stir them into action. These poems can be read in the quiet at home. Almost all bring revival to the fore. Messages are aimed at the heart of every person.

Out of the blue? No, my belief is that the Lord set me into action in an extraordinary way. You see, first I wrote a book of church cartoons, *Laugh with the Lord* then an autobiography, *The Road to Jesus Is Never Closed.* They both were seemingly out of the blue, yet I am sure they were inspired by our wonderful Lord. Then I received the urge to write poetry, and I found it hard to stop. In fact, so far I have written over five hundred poems, all with evangelical flavors.

All these poems release from me my desire to tell everyone about Jesus, no holds barred. Jesus lives and loves, and every one of us must bring folk to know Jesus.

Go through the great variety of titles; every one leads to Jesus. The basic message is "Follow Jesus" said in countless ways. It is my fervent prayer that these poems will pull at the heartstrings of many who read them.

Church leaders are wonderfully dedicated, saintly people. Yet their churches are often lacking in members. They need the Holy Spirit to awaken in them the need to evangelize, to bring people to accept Jesus, to save lives. The need for those in the pews to take on new life is urgently required. It can happen; to God, nothing is impossible. These poems can help point the way.

Revival can be done by having enthusiasm that is contagious and sets each church on fire.

These poems are meant for all: unbelievers, telling them what they are missing; fence sitters, hoping they will come to Jesus; pew-sitting Christians, telling them gently but firmly that they need to move into action for Jesus; and the truly dedicated, helping them in their sacrificial work. These poems are meant for pastors too. We can all learn; we can all realize that we can do better. The dedicated worship leader can read out many of the poems to those assembled andthen even copy them and give them out as keepsakes. *Hallelujah!*

Contents

This Book is dedicated to my Daughter

ESTHER

My thanks and appreciation to the Publishing Staff

Inspiring Voices for their advice and help.

ACTION THIS DAY

Do you belong
To a church?
One with committees?
Almost for sure!
How much action
Comes each month
From each committee?
To become vibrant,
Forget committees!
Place one person in charge
Of each ministry,
Authorized to act,
To delegate tasks,
And then to make, each month,
A short progress report
Of what has been done.
Or there may be
A committee with a deadline
After which it goes.
Picture a rubber stamp.
All it says is,

"Action This Day."
Think how your church
Will advance,
Will accomplish,
Will succeed
In many spheres.
Think of the way
Former committee members
Can be used
With new ministries,
New targets,
New results.
Brush away
All the cobwebs;
Prepare for the change.
You will open
A new chapter
Of unseen accomplishments,
And you will never look back.
Use Action This Day!
Hallelujah!

ALMOST SAVED

Countless thousands
Have become
Halfway Christians,
Or have found the way
Too tough,
Then turned back
To their easier ways,
Ways that end
In eternal hell.
Almost persuaded
Means very simply
Turning your back
On Jesus the Saviour.
It means that you have
No spiritual stamina,
No real backbone,
No real idea
Of what you are missing.
You've turned away from
Real happiness,
Being on fire
With enthusiasm,

With eagerness,
With the desire
To bring others
To Jesus, your Lord.
You've forgotten
There are only two roads:
One to heaven
And one to hell.
There is time to change,
And the time is now.
Find a private place,
Make your decision.
Give yourself utterly,
And you will,
With His help,
No longer be an "almost"
But a living follower
Of Jesus, your friend.
Do it right now.
There is no other time.
Halleluhah!

AT SEA

Have you ever been to sea?
It really is an experience
To sail upon the ocean,
Out of sight of land,
To look around
And see just the sea,
It makes our thoughts
Go directly
To God's creation
To realize that the seas
Cover over half the world.
Then at night on the sea,
The skies seem even larger.
Looking up to see
Countless twinkling stars.
The sea and the skies,
The greatness of creation.
And the message to the heart
Is of wonderful peace,
That God is in charge
Of the waters and the sky
Of His world.

No man can have made
Such wondrous sights.
Nor the fishes of the sea,
Nor the birds of the air.
Yet so many people are blind.
They see those stars,
They sea the sea
Without a thought
Of God's majesty.
God deserves
So much more
And to have such blindness
Swept away.
Our witness,
Our testimony,
Ourselves, we
Must go to work,
His work.
Thank you, Lord,
For your creation.
Help us show others
Your wonders,
Especially those
Who do not see.
Thank you, Lord,
Hallelujah!

BACKSEAT DRIVER

When you drive your car,
Do you have
A backseat driver?
You know the sort—
"Mind that cyclist,"
"Don't drive too fast,"
"Drive more carefully,"
And so much more!
Your backseat driver
May even be
Your nearest and dearest.
Expressing—overexpressing—
Care and concern.
Speaking thoughts.
It can be most annoying,
But usually done
With much good intent.
Switch over
From the usual
Back-seat driver
Who strives to keep you
Safe and sound.
There is another
Back-seat driver,
A very important one,
For your whole life.
He's great,
He's positive,
He's your friend,

The Lord Jesus Christ.
Such a great difference!
He's your spiritual guide.
Jesus shows you the way,
Truly your navigator.
He tells you
How to steer your life,
To tell others of His love,
To be fishers of souls,
To love your neighbor,
To sow the seeds.
Bring more to Him;
He never, never leaves you.
He does not tell you
Just what you must do.
He walks with you,
Directs you.
He is your constant comrade.
Why the backseat driver?
Because you drive your life,
And like all drivers,
You are not perfect.
You really do need
The best backseat driver
To be sure you drive God's way.
Remember, you can drive,
But put Christ in charge;
Drive His way.
Hallelujah!

BEING LATE

You know,
Some people
Think it's too late
To be born again.
They've got to be told
Jesus made it clear
That those who come last
Are just as welcome
As those who came
Many years before.
Those early ones,
Those later ones are all equal
In the sight of God.
For those who witness,
It is vital always
To bring the elderly to Jesus,
For God loves
Both the young and the old.

Being late
Seemingly seems
To be a slight
Or a disadvantage.
Remember Jesus' parable.
It is your answer,
It is your sign,
It is your target.
All—everyone—
Treat as VIPs,
God's VIPs.
Serving the Lord is great!
Exciting and an adventure.
So thank the Lord,
Be guided by prayer,
Your search for all
Will succeed.
Hallelujah!

BEING QUIET

It's always being said,
Especially in the Bible,
To find a place
To talk to God.
A quiet place,
A private place.
A place free from noise.
That helps bring you
Closer to God.
This is hard at times.
Perhaps a spouse
Who does not understand.
Perhaps the ringing
Of a telephone.
Martin Luther
Found peace and refuge
In a coal shed to pray!
We, in this modern age,
May have to walk in a park,
Down a country lane,
Or just to within
A garden shed
To be entirely alone.
To spend real time
With the Lord.
Real time
Aims at stopping clocks,
The sound of voices,
And all distractions.

Then, when alone,
That real prayer,
That sacred time,
Will be yours with Jesus.
Thank Him,
Ask forgiveness,
Tell Him your concerns.
But do not forget
To pause and listen.
Do not have
One-way prayer.
Be ready for directions.
Be ready for guidance,
For prayer goes two ways.
If the mind wanders,
Pull back by saying "Jesus"
And repeating that precious name.
Picture Him,
Maybe with the children,
Maybe on the Mount,
Or on the cross,
And listen again to Him,
Then back to talking,
Friend to friend.
That quiet time,
Truly real time,
Will be blessed.
Hallelujah!

BIBLES

Almost every house
Has a Bible,
The Word of God.
Again, almost all
Are rarely or never read.
Strange, for it is a treasure
More valuable
Than any passport!
Yet God's Word is ignored.
The Word of God,
The truest of words.
God is our Father,
Jesus, His Son.
Then Jesus was crucified
To show God's love
For all of us.
And Jesus rose from the dead,
Seen by hundreds,

One day to return.
Then a thousand more truths.
There is an answer
To every doubt.
There are promises
For all who read.
The Word of God
Gives you life
In His eternity.
For those
Who leave the Bible untouched,
Sadly, their future
Will end in grief.
Pick up your Bible.
Use it every day.
Discover that love.
Believe it forever!
Hallelujah!

BIRTHDAYS

We all have a birthday,
A time to celebrate,
Especially to celebrate
When we are young.
Did you know
About a second birthday?
A much, much bigger day?
When we were born,
Our life of eternity began;
That was birthday number one.
Then when we die,
That marks
Birthday number two!
That really is true.
Birthday number two
Is the biggest,
The most important.
It's your entry day
Into heaven or hell.
There are no more

Second chances.
What you have done
In all of your life
Decides your destiny.
For a believer,
Your second birthday,
It is glorious,
It is exciting,
Unspeakable.
So many do not know
About their second birthday!
The entry into
The Promised Land.
The time to meet Jesus,
The time of reunions,
Of real celebration.
Be sure you are prepared
For that wonderful day
Hallelujah!

BREAD MAKING

Have you ever made bread?
Smelled fresh-made bread?
Tasted fresh-made bread?
So much tastier
Than superstore bread.
Many who make their own
Use a bread machine.
Hand kneading is best.
Mix the ingredients,
Then knead and knead
Ten minutes nonstop.
Let it rest;
The yeast will rise and rise.
Then knead again.
Magically marvellous!
The Bible tells us of bread—
So many times,
And of yeast.

Jesus said that he was
The Bread of Life.
At the Last Supper
The bread was His body.
Bread is our basic food.
Physically and spiritually
Every one of us
Needs bread.
At your next meal
And at every meal
Where bread is eaten,
Think of biblical bread
And give thanks to God.
Do not take bread for granted;
It comes from God.
We cannot do without it.
Hallelujah!

BREAKING NEWS

"Breaking News" on TV
Means new news coming in,
A news flash.
It's the latest,
It's right up to date,
It's brand new.
News that often is not good.
News that, like the rest,
Fades away, usually in days.
Usually to be forgotten.
At the other end
Of real reality
Is news eternal.
This lasts forever;
It can never fade.
The gospel is good news.
It was breaking news

Two thousand years ago,
And this news is still fresh!
The news that saves,
The news that rescues,
That changes lives
These very days.
News that is strong,
Powerful,
And never mundane.
Incomparable
With anything else.
Real news,
Up to date.
News that must be shared.
It is priceless news:
Jesus lives!
Hallelujah!

BROKEN DOWN

So many things go wrong.
Heated words
To ones you love.
Misunderstandings,
Dead end ways,
Wasted days.
Self at the front,
God pushed behind.
Even words profane
And acts gone wrong.
Down in the depths
Down into darkness.
Then I recalled
That in the past
God came first.
Even now
He would forgive.
The Lord can lift us.
Any who pray
Are lifted up

From the pit of despair.
He sets our feet
On firm ground.
He steadies us as we walk.
Read that in Jeremiah.
The way becomes clear
As we step into His Way,
Love Him
And put Him first
In everything.
He has erased those sins,
All things are new.
The sun shines,
His light shines,
The fire of His love
Warms us through and through.
No more life in tatters,
God is here to stay,
And the Devil fled.
Hallelujah!

BROWNIE POINTS

You work hard for Jesus.
You show dedication.
You do well,
You do very well,
And God is pleased
At the seed you sowed.
Do you remember
That what we do
And all that we do
Is what is expected
When we serve the Lord?
But be clear:
Christians do not collect
Brownie points!
Our service for Jesus
Can never equal
What Jesus has done
For all of mankind.
Good works
Go hand in hand

With faith in Jesus
"Service" sounds better
Than saying "Works"!
Service includes sharing,
Sharing the good news
With everyone.
This in turn is love
And love needs no points!
Love gives out
All of the time.
It's wonderful
That do-ers
Have no points.
So much more is gained
Just in winning,
Winning souls for Jesus.
Thank you, Lord,
For this privilege.
Hallelujah!

CAMBODIAN TRAFFIC

You have to see it
To believe it!
The nonstop traffic,
Literally nonstop!
Never, never
Expect the traffic to stop
At pedestrian crossings.
They won't,
They will speed on.
It seems as if
All have urgent business!
Cars, lorries, vans,
Motorbikes
That carry three or more,
All worshipping speed,
Come what may.
One way to cross
Is to follow closely
A local pedestrian
On his aim to cross—
Or not to cross at all.
Or wait for a gridlock.
This chaotic traffic
Is so much like
The lives many live.
We go full tilt,

Regardless,
Wrapped in ourselves.
Little or no thought for others.
We speed past all others.
And we hurry
Without reason to hurry.
It is time to change.
It's time to realize
That life is much greater
When we unwrap ourselves.
Share yourselves
And you'll receive from others.
You're opening up
To receive God's bounty.
You've a lot to give,
And a lot to receive,
Slow down.
Take time with God,
That fast pace is over.
Don't come to a halt,
For there is much to do,
In God's time, not yours.
Life is great,
Much better
Than at full speed!
Hallelujah!

CHILIES ARE HOT

In the Western world,
The taste for chilies
Is just beginning.
Chilies chopped up,
Chilies powdered,
Chilies ground with prawns
All to liven
Any savory dish.
For some,
Even desserts!
Chilies give zest and life
To the dullest of food.
Why all this
About cookery?
Because it is the same
When we look at ourselves.
It is identical
When we accept Jesus.
Our lives had been
Colorless, useless.
Then Jesus comes in.
Our lives
Become full of spice.
Full of vigour,
Full of joy.

Yes, born again!
Brand new people!
He warms our hearts,
He sets us on fire,
He keeps aglow
Forever and ever.
We become eager,
We are enthusiastic,
We are dedicated.
It leaves those chilies
Way in the shade!
What a change!
What a difference!
And still not finished.
Being on fire for Jesus
Means bringing fire
To others.
Fiery prayers
And fiery heights.
Spread that fire,
Bring others to know
What Jesus can do
In all their lives.
May your flames last forever.
Hallelujah!

CHRISTIAN MULTIPLICATION

The words *Christian Multiplication*
Come from Bill Bright's
Witness Without Fear.
It's a good way in following Jesus.
A way, that if followed,
Followed to the letter,
Would convert a whole country,
Probably even the world,
In a lifetime.
Each Christian
As Jesus instructed
Brings another to Christ.
Then the new believer,
Filled with the Holy Spirit,
Testifies, witnesses
And brings another to Christ.
In turn this new believer
Brings yet another to Christ.
One person starts it,
Then there are two,
Then it goes to four.
Four bring four more,
Then to eight and sixteen.
Thirty-two and more,
And more and more and more.

It's mind boggling!
Yet it is doing simply
What Jesus tells us to do.
"Be fishers of men."
Just think of a small church.
If each of ten members
Brought to Christ
Ten unbelievers,
The church would double in size.
Then just another drive
And the church would be
Quadrupled!
It is not impossible,
Nothing is impossible
With God.
We must, in every church,
Resolve before God
To be inflamed, spurred on
Through the Holy Spirit,
To aim and work this way.
Flatten obstacles
Head for new targets
And rejoice in victory.
Hallelujah!

CLUELESS CROWDS

Wherever you go,
Crowds throng,
Unending streams.
To shop sales,
To football and sports,
Aimlessly to anything
That may be exciting
And break through the boredom.
It's a continual search.
Come out of the crowds!
There is a far better way,
A permanent way
Never to be bored again!
So much more to be gained
By changing your life.
By finding adventures,
By being excited,
By gaining happiness,
Satisfaction,
Enthusiasm.
It starts by going to church.
Maybe the one you passed
So many times.

It can be your entry
Into everlasting life!
Get clued up!
Get filled with Jesus
And the Holy Spirit.
You will be turned
Upside down!
Altered completely,
And Jesus is the reason.
Nobody else can change us
As Jesus can do.
We see with new eyes,
With new ears,
With new feelings,
With a new heart.
Then join those crowds again,
This time differently.
To tell of His love,
Life-changing for all.
It's a mission for life
And life for all.
Thank you, Lord.
Hallelujah!

COUNTING BLESSINGS

Have you ever counted
All your blessings
That God has given?
Or when you pray
Is it like a grocery list?
Or as it should be,
A time of thanksgiving?
Get paper and pen,
Write down
All of your blessings,
One by one.
It's amazing,
It's fantastic,
It's far more than thought,
What God has done
And done with no thanks!
So thank Him now
And use that list,
Adding to it
As the Lord gives more.
Blessings differ
From person to person.
Go back on your life,
Right to the times

Of your childhood.
The list gets longer,
Without those blessings
What a terrible life
It would have been!
List down the mountain tops,
The valleys,
The illnesses,
The depressions,
The celebrations,
A real mixed bag,
Yet coming through
You spot the blessings,
Yes, God is good
All the time!
We've all been blessed,
Hundreds of times!
It shows you
Jesus' love for you.
It shows you
You were never alone,
And you never will be!
Hallelujah!

DECISIONS, DECISIONS

Most of us
Are pretty restless.
We seem to be
Always on the go.
Life seems so full
Of stress.
Too many decisions—
"Mend this,"
"Mend that,"
"Phone Mr. Jones,"
"Find a dentist,"
"Pick a time to meet."
And so much more!
How to let go?
Stop everything!
Sit down,
Close your eyes,
Cup your hands,
And pray!
"Dear Jesus,

I'm sorry I forgot you!
I'm going to ask You
For Help
And for support.
For help
For everything I do.
Sorry, Lord,
For leaving You out!"
Already you feel more settled,
More at peace,
More able
More prepared.
Get up and go,
Not by yourself,
But hand in hand
With Jesus.
"Thank You, Jesus,
I'm ready now
For all I have to do."
Hallelujah!

DEEP DEPRESSION

Do you know
Real depression?
Real blackness?
Recurring every day?
It is scary,
It is at your wits' end.
But even then there is Jesus.
It's true!
But you must have faith,
Believe He is there.
It's true,
And you'll know,
When you pray
The hardest you ever prayed.
Don't feel alone,
Jesus is with you.
Then there is more.
You may need your doctor,
Perhaps a specialist,
For depression
Is an illness,
One that can be treated.
It can be controlled,
Often cleared.
Take it to Jesus,
For He will help
Along with those
Whom he blessed

With skills.
I've been there—
It is indescribable,
But the Lord
And His servants
Brought me through.
Fit to write,
Fit to witness,
Fit to Lead,
And life is full.
Full of happiness,
Full of joy,
Full of everything!
You have that big "D"?
Be assured,
Jesus first,
Then His helpers
And with your prayers
The light will be seen.
Do not despair,
Jesus is there,
Waiting for you
To pray.
When it's all over,
Be sure to testify,
Be sure to help others
Out of the pit of despair.
Hallelujah!

DENYING JESUS

Peter denied Christ
Three times
But lived to serve Jesus
Until he died.
How many times
Have you and I
Denied our Lord?
We have all done this.
We deny Him
When we accept
The secular world.
Every dishonest act,
Every time we lie,
Every time we argue,
And so much more.
When we go our way
And not the Jesus way.

We may not want to deny
It's thoughtlessness.
We are guilty
And we need to confess,
To pray.
We need to ask forgiveness
For wrongs we have done.
Then follow Peter,
Go out and witness.
Shed denials,
Be certain to tell
Jesus' love is for all.
Be cleansed of the past,
Share the joy,
It's great,
Never stop your praise.
Hallelujah!

DEVILS ARE REAL

There are some who believe
That there is no Devil!
They cannot see
Beyond their noses!
There are two ways,
The bad way
And the good way.
The good way leads with love,
Stems from our Savior.
The bad has one source,
The Devil.
Even Jesus fought
With the Devil.
"Get thee behind me," He said.
Every bad thought,
Every bad action,
Delights the Devil.
Temptation

Is one of his weapons.
We must follow Jesus
And fight the Devil.
Real heartfelt prayer
Defeats the Devil
Every time.
The Devil knows weak spots.
No one, no one at all
Can say
That the Devil leaves him alone.
But we can testify
How we win our battles
When such trials come.
Be sure to arm yourself,
Ready at all times
To fend off evils.
You'll be victorious!
Hallelujah!

DIETING

Have you ever thought
Of dieting?
Most adults
In their forties
And upwards
Need to lose pounds
To regain a reasonable look,
To regain reasonable health.
So start a diet.
You find you need
Discipline,
Steadfastness,
The will to succeed.
Alas, many fail.
Some try several times
And end on square one.
That need not be!
Have discipline and win.
It's just the same way
For a greater life.
Take a spiritual diet.
You may realize
You've slackened off!
You've let go,

Forgot to pray,
Not gone to church
And gradually,
Almost sprouting horns!
You've lost your discipline
You've even lost
Good Christian friends.
Get down to prayer,
Return to His Word,
Return to your church.
Back comes fellowship,
Back comes friends,
Back comes fitness,
Spiritual fitness.
Your regular worship
Blossoms into
Regular service for Jesus.
No more need to diet,
You are full,
Full of the Holy Spirit.
Life is back to real life.
You've got tough,
Tough for Jesus.
Hallelujah!

DO A U-TURN

U-turns are special.
In a car rarely done.
In our lives
Just as rare.
For those who love Christ
There is a problem.
The problem is
To have those
To whom they witness
Do U-turns.
To have the nonbeliever
Become a red-hot believer
And such a U-turn
Is a hard thing to do.
Those folk live lives
They have set
Almost in concrete.
We have to start with prayer,
With faith.
We have to know
Our strength is Jesus.
Those who are changed

Are changed
By the Holy Spirit.
Not by our puny efforts.
U-turns are done this way.
We plant the seed
And pray for growth.
Each U-turn,
Each move to Jesus
Is a miracle.
Try your hardest
And pray to be led
To help those U-turn,
To know that miracles
Happen every day.
Yes, U-turns are special,
Each Christian is special.
Join in the drive
To create U-turns
This week,
This month
And all the time!
Hallelujah!

DOS AND DON'TS

A lot of people think
We belong to
To "The Don't Brigade."
"Don't swear."
"Don't drink."
"Don't bet."
"Don't cheat."
And a lot lot more.
Of course, some are wrong,
Very wrong,
And truthfully,
Life would shine
Without swearing,
Without drinking,
Without gambling,
And without cheating.
More factually,
Christians are full of "Dos."
"Do help the needy,"
"Do care for the sick,"

"Do love your neighbor,"
"Do witness to others,"
And many more.
Then there are good "Don'ts."
"Don't cheat" makes sense.
"Don't ignore others."
"Don't be a hypocrite."
"Don't judge."
Christians are different.
We must be positive,
We must be adventurous,
We must tell others
That Jesus loves all,
That life is good.
It's a glorious life,
A victorious life,
A life
With everlasting future.
Make sure we share this.
Hallelujah!

DON'T TOUCH ASBESTOS

Years ago,
Asbestos was used
To protect us from fire.
Now it is known
As toxic to our bodies.
No longer used,
It is torn down.
Destroyed.
The Lord gives free choice,
Free will to all,
But it's a bit like asbestos.
Your decisions
Come from yourselves.
To those without Christ
Choices are often toxic.
They can disrupt,
They can destroy,
They can contaminate.
It is only
When Christ dwells within

That decisions do not harm.
Yes, you have free will.
So like asbestos,
Throw away bad habits,
Destroy evil ways.
Have all you do
God-led.
Decision time
Links with prayer time.
The self-choice,
The free will
Is God-given,
Use it His way
Not your way.
Thank you, Lord,
For helping us know
Decisions are special
When led by you.
Hallelujah!

DOUBTING THOMAS

Almost everyone
Has been a Doubting Thomas.
Thomas could not believe
That Jesus was alive.
He had to have proof.
These days, every person
Who accepts Jesus
Comes in faith.
There is no proof
Such as Thomas had.
And we do have doubts
To some degree.
About answers to prayer,
About miracles,
About the reality,
Of all we know.
Doubts?
Yes, we had them,
Several!
But as we grew
In knowing Jesus,

We felt the presence
Of the Holy Spirit,
The comforter within us.
The Bible tells us
Many times
Faith is the key,
The key to belief.
Faith melts away
Doubts that were there.
Faith rules
And God rules.
And we follow Him.
No more do we doubt,
Christ indeed is risen,
And we wonder now
Why we ever doubted!
We know
We are sure.
Doubts have fled,
We are with Jesus!
Hallelujah!

EXERCISING WITH GOD

We all know
That exercise is good.
It keeps us fit,
It gives us strength,
Physical strength.
Ever thought further?
Of spiritual fitness?
Far more important.
A daily devotion
And a short prayer
Is not enough!
It's far too little!
Brother Lawrence, years ago,
Working in the kitchen
In his monastery,
Cleaning pots and pans
And scrubbing floors.
He was spiritually fit
From top to toe.
It was said that his praying
And his working
Were joined together.
He talked with God
And he continued talking

While he worked
Amongst the dirty dishes.
He was one with God.
All day long.
This is the way,
For everyone.
Sure, have prayer time,
Then when working
Don't let go of God.
When shopping,
When walking from A to B,
When preparing meals
Or doing housework
He can be just as close.
Walk the walk,
Talk the talk with Jesus.
Have your gym,
Have your exercise,
Pray then!
Keep fit,
Mind and Body,
They go together.
Hallelujah!

EXCUSES GALORE

You say you're a Christian.
You do go to church.
Even attend meetings.
But are you really right?
Or laden with excuses?
Excuses about meager giving,
Excuses on reading books
That glorify secular sex.
Excuses on watching TV
Unfit for any to see.
Excuses on minor wrongs.
"Oh, this is normal,
Done by all!"
You think you must not be
Narrow-minded!
Your thinking and doing
Is wrong, very wrong!
Just think,
If Jesus knocked at your door,
Would you say
And think the same?

Or would you wish
To show your Sunday self!
We cannot have two faces.
We must be fully for Jesus
Or we are not Christians.
Think right now—
Jesus is not just knocking,
He is within your home.
He knows your thoughts,
He sees your actions.
There are no excuses,
All are unacceptable.
Therefore, it is time
To seek forgiveness,
Then turn to a new leaf
And a new life.
Do this right now,
There is no better time.
He waits for you
For He loves you.
Hallelujah!

FAITH

To believe in Jesus,
To be a Christian,
There is a problem.
We have to have faith!
That is the problem,
Faith!
Think, though,
Do we ever use faith
In our daily lives?
Yes, we do!
Many times,
Sometimes daily.
Do you cycle?
How do you balance?
With faith, of course!
When we travel by air
What do we have?
Faith, of course,
Faith in the pilot!
If we have an operation,
What must we have?
Faith, of course,
In the surgeon,
That he has been trained.
Almost unknowingly
Faith fills our lives.

So really,
To anyone with sense,
There should be no problem
In having faith
To be a Christian!
In having faith
That Jesus
Is the Son of God.
That He is with us,
And He is Lord.
No problem at all!
Bear in mind, though,
The Bible says
"Faith goes with works."
So Christians must believe
With full faith
And then know
Action is also needed.
Jesus never idled,
Nor must we.
Therefore rejoice,
Rejoice in a new life,
Wonderfully blessed
And full of faith.
Hallelujah!

FEAST OR FAST?

When you drive with Jesus,
Truly following Him,
There is no automatic gear!
Running on automatic
Is far too easy.
We have to have
A manual gear,
Gear we can control
On the way we drive.
Christians on automatic
Have lost their way.
They think they've done enough.
No more effort is needed.
They are in the lazy gear.
The end of a good life.
Those on manual are feasting,
Feasting on joy,
Feasting on adventure,
On positive happenings.
Jesus set a feast for all.
In His parables
The sort of person
On the automatic
Were Sadducees and Pharisees.
While those on manual

Were the less perfect,
And they filled the table
When the Lord had a feast.
The others had to fast!
Serving the Lord
Means controlling
That manual gear.
More to do
And more to have.
Can anything be enjoyed
More than loving Jesus?
No!
For the nondoers,
Those in the lazy gear,
The future is bleak,
It's a permanent fast.
For our manual folk,
Pure doses of eagerness
Of enthusiasm.
The sort
That contagiously infects—
Hopefully the lazy ones!
Fast or feast?
You know which!
Hallelujah!

FOLLOW THE SON

God sent His Son
To show His ways.
He loves us so much
That he allowed His Son
To be mocked and scourged
And then crucified.
And then in three days
To rise from the dead.
Why, oh, why is it
That billions fail to see this?
To follow Jesus
As their Saviour?
What fools are they!
They worship themselves
And the glare and the glitter
Of the secular world.
There is only one way,
God's way.
And His way
Must be shown to others.

We must ask our Lord
To direct our paths.
To give us courage
To open our mouths.
It is our bounden duty
To be fishers of souls.
To try each day
To turn lives around.
To follow His Son.
There are no exceptions
To doing what Jesus
Has told us to do.
His finger points
To you and to me.
Thank God for His Son,
Be resolved to obey,
It's the Jesus way,
It must be yours!
Hallelujah!

FROZEN CHOSEN

One Sunday
I sat in my pew.
The preacher asked a question.
"Are you a frozen chosen?"
He went on to explain.
"Do you come to church
Most Sundays?
Do you pray only a little?
Do you skip daily devotions?"
He seemed to point a finger
Right at me.
He seemed to look
Right through me.
What he said was what I did.
Then he enlarged
On what he said.
That that way
We were in a rut.
That we just believed
And just sat back.
We were the frozen chosen.
We were asked,
Did the disciples just sit back?

If Andrew had not witnessed,
What would have happened?
If Zaccheus had stayed up the tree,
How would things have changed?
If Paul had ignored
The call at Damascus,
We might not today
Have been Christians.
So should we just sit
In our little pews?
The message went on
To be doers of His Word.
To decide right now,
Not tomorrow,
Not next week!
We were told
After the service
To report for duty!
Out of the rut
And onto the crest
Of a mighty wave!
Hallelujah!

GARDENING

Christians are gardeners.
Just imagine
A rough plot of land.
Then we willingly dig,
Turning the earth,
Preparing it
To receive good seed.
What sort of seed?
It's God's seeds.
Seeds to bring people
To know Jesus.
Only after much work
Are seeds ready to sow.
Each seed is prepared
With so much effort.
Witnessing,
Praying, and talking,
Meeting hostility,
And persevering.

It takes courage,
It takes conviction
And dedication
Before the seed is sown.
And then it must be left
For God to tend and water
To bring to maturity.
To bring to harvest.
More people are needed
To witness,
To prepare the seed,
Doers of His Word.
Christians must become
Out-looking,
Moving into action.
Get digging,
Go prepare,
Then plant the seed!
Hallelujah!

GET ON YOUR BIKE

It's an English saying,
"Get on your bike!"
Simply means
"Get into action!"
In other words,
Don't hang about.
Do something.
Be something.
It is a phrase
For every Christian,
No exceptions
Whatsoever.
After all,
It is biblical.
To be doers of the Word,
Fishers of souls,
For everyone
To follow Christ.
Not just by believing,
That is not enough,
But by action.
No one can be a Christian
By just believing

And leaving God's commands
To others.
The Bible tells us
Faith and works
Makes the Christian.
Just believing without works
Is selfish,
Shows lack of courage.
God knows all your thoughts,
Knows whether you serve
Or whether not.
Why you do not serve,
And sadly why you are idle.
Be aware and turn about,
Show your Father
Your change of mind.
You will be blessed.
Those around you,
And your church
Will be the stronger.
On your bike!
Hallelujah!

GET SAVED

Are you a "surface Christian"?
Or are you soaked
With the Holy Spirit?
Are you lukewarm
Or on fire for Jesus?
Being soaked
Means through and through,
No holds barred.
Your aim—
To be a real disciple.
To consider each day
Would be ill-spent
If nothing is done
To advance the kingdom.
Being a disciple
Has no limits.
So keen as to be contagious.
To be able to spread
All enthusiasm to others.

To change the tepid
To boiling hot.
From frozen chosen
To born again.
Be a warrior,
Fight for Jesus,
Rescue the unsaved.
Be at war with evil,
At meaningless messages.
Pull the sinking
From pits of despair.
Show them the joy
That can be their own.
Never give up,
Let "Get saved"
Be your great aim
With all you can meet.
Great is the reward.
Hallelujah!

GIANTS

Giants can be small!
David was a giant,
A boy facing Goliath.
In our present age,
There is a boy
In Somalia.
He loved Jesus.
Pagans took him,
Nailed legs and feet
To wooden planks
And he was left to die.
But his friends found him,
He recovered.
He told his friend,
"I forgive those men.
Jesus forgave those
Who nailed Him to a cross.
I should do the same."
A boy that was a giant.
There are many giants
Amongst Christians.

When you witness,
You become a giant.
It takes courage and faith.
When you say a prayer
For the first time.
Before your friends,
You become a giant.
Many Christian giants
Are never known.
But Jesus knows each one.
Name by name.
Help us all, Lord,
To be giants for you.
Whatever are status,
Rich or poor,
Educated or not,
Whatever our race,
Please make us giants,
Giants for You.
Hallelujah!

GLOW, GROW, GO

Have you heard of the three Gs?
Glow, Grow, and Go.
Jesus said,
"Let your light shine,"
So start with Glow!
Some have said,
"God made round faces
And men made them long."
But filled by the Spirit,
You just have to Glow!
When you glow
It is often spread.
See that it does!
Then comes Grow.
This is when you mature.
You have valleys,
You have peaks,
The tougher you get
The greater the growth.
No Christian life
Is smooth all the time.

It's the dips and the downs
That give you more growth.
So you Glow,
And you Grow.
And the final word is Go.
Go into every place
To spread the good news.
Be real fishers of souls.
The news of Jesus' love,
The news that every man,
Every woman and child
Is loved by God.
Go tell and plant the seed.
Glow, Grow, Go.
It is not just for you,
It's a challenge to all,
Especially your church.
Don't just read this,
Do something,
Plant.
God will water.
Hallelujah!

GOD'S COMPUTER

Not all that long ago
Computers were unknown.
The best computer
Was—and is—the brain.
Even today, our brains
Have memories unsurpassed,
Better than any computer.
How on earth
Can a humanist
Fail to realize,
That every thought
Must come from God's computer?
Whatever scientists can do,
They will never, never
Beat God's computer.
Indeed, every effort
Stems from God Himself.
From the brain.

The atheist,
The doubter,
Seem completely blind
When they fail to know
That they are God-made.
It is incredible,
Unbelievable,
Hardly understood,
The great God-made brain.
How would we know
Our Maker,
Our Savior,
His wonderful love
Without our brains!
Thank you, Lord,
You're unbeatable!
Hallelujah!

GOD AT YOUR DOOR

Have you ever seen
The picture of Jesus
Wearing a crown of thorns
And knocking
At a door?
It's a famous scene
Taken from the Bible,
"I stand at the door
And knock."
It's your door,
Everyone's door.
The door of every church.
Realize,
Not even once in history
Has Jesus
Forced His way in.
He gives free will,
And in this way decide.
We have to choose
Whether to open the door.
Or to ignore His call.
That crown of thorns
Shows of His great love,
His sacrifice for all.
Open the door
And it's the way to life,
Eventual paradise.

Why be so foolish
As to reject Christ?
And in that way
Enter eternal hell?
It's much the same,
Even for churches!
Too many fail to serve.
To have
Comfortable Christianity.
No evangelizing,
Almost beyond
Any understanding.
Churches are duty-bound
To open their door,
To strive in every fiber
To advance
His kingdom.
Comfortable Christianity
Is a nonstarter.
Pray without ceasing
That every church
Will serve the Lord
With might and mane.
Acceptable to Jesus
In joyful strength.
Hallelujah!

GOD'S COMMANDS

God's commands—
How to explain
Just what they are.
Basically,
It's common sense!
We know within us
That we must not kill,
Steal, cheat, swear,
That adultery is wrong,
Greed is not good,
Jealousy and envy
Have no place.
Our conscience
Is a litmus paper.
We just know
Right from wrong.
But there are additions.
Jesus said,
To love your neighbour
As much as yourself.
That real love
Is essential in everything.
It shows a cycle.
With love, you never want
To kill, steal, swear, cheat,

And do other wrongs.
Love rules your life.
Then Jesus told us
To go the second mile.
That is love again!
Doing the second mile
Brings joy to all,
You feel you float
Upon a great big cloud!
God's commands,
They make sense.
They do not blot out
Fun and merriment.
Fact is, your fun
Becomes even greater!
Following God's commands
Brings a good life
Right to the hilt.
Thank the Lord
For His directions,
For taking you along
God's road,
The road that leads to paradise.
Hallelujah!

GOD IS HERE

"God is here."
Remember these three words.
Hold them in your heart,
They are so special.
It brings a smile.
In good times
And in bad times
These words give strength.
When in a valley
Those words can lift,
Lift you upward.
Many are those
Who have depression.
Then cling to those words.
Do not let go,
They are lifesavers.
Believe totally that
"God is here."

Keep repeating these words,
Even then, it's hard.
Then turn to prayer,
And with faith,
End with "God is here."
Your resolve will emerge,
Your fight to climb
Out from despair
Will begin to work.
Keep your eyes upon Jesus,
Keep talking to Him.
Know you are not alone.
Then praise Him,
Then thank Him,
You will be back,
Back on firm ground.
Hallelujah!

GOOGLE WORLD

The wonders of the Internet
Bring so much of everything!
There is Google Earth.
With proper know-how,
You find your town,
Then your street,
And even your house,
All on your own computer.
Nothing is hidden,
It's all revealed.
Try again overseas!
It's just the same
All over the world.
Hold on, though.
Spiritually,
God is more powerful.
More than Google
And others websites.
He beams down upon all.
He knows our names,
He knows our thoughts,
He even knows
What we will say

Before we speak.
Nothing is hidden
The good, the bad,
All is known.
He knows each person
Inside out.
Our hopes,
Our weaknesses,
Our aims.
If we really want Jesus
You can be sure of help,
Be sure of cleansing,
Be sure of direction,
Be sure of salvation.
But remember, He knows you,
Inside out.
False followers
Cannot survive.
Just love Jesus,
Utterly, completely,
You'll win the race!
Hallelujah!

GRASSROOTS

The best Christians
Are grassroots Christians.
Those who work,
Those who serve.
Those who witness
At ground level.
The sort of person
Who avoids committees.
He has too much to do!
The real work of any church
Is at grassroots level.
Move higher up,
You have less time
To actually serve,
To accomplish His Will.
Even in churches,
Regrettably,
There can be politics.
Down at grassroots level

You are down to earth.
You are face to face
With those who need help.
To the unbeliever,
To the folk with problems.
There are no debates,
No discussions.
There is counseling,
There are actions,
There are decisions made.
It's frontline service.
One little thought.
Did Jesus hold committees?
There wasn't time!
Nor should there be
For those
At grassroots level!
Hallelujah!

HAVE A MINISTRY

Get yourself a ministry!
What does that mean?
It means a regular job
For your Savior, Jesus.
In the Book of Revelations,
We are called priests.
This means all of us
Should have ministries!
Ministries are many.
From cleaning brasses,
Dusting the pews,
Arranging flowers,
Welcoming worshippers,
Especially newcomers,
Behind the scenes catering,
Tending church gardens.
Then there is the choir—
Or starting one!
Sunday school teaching,
And so much more.

All for Jesus.
You already have a ministry?
Well done! Start another!
A prayer cell,
Visiting the sick and elderly,
The list is without end.
Regretfully,
So many do so little.
Jesus always served others,
Even washing feet.
He set the example
For us all to follow.
The more who serve,
The stronger the church.
Keep at it,
You are important,
You are needed.
Thank the Lord
And take that ministry!
Hallelujah!

HELL? NO!

I've heard it said
There is no hell,
It does not exist.
Believe me, it does exist.
I've been there.
I've even met the Devil.
True—just a foretaste,
And enough for anyone.
Hell will be eternal
For those who never heed.
I was in the pit,
Desperate and in despair.
I prayed and prayed
To Jesus
The One I had ignored.
There were no miracles,
But in the dark tunnel,

Claustrophobic,
A glimmer of light,
A light to follow,
A light that brightened.
And the darkness lifted.
I was away from evilness.
I was approaching Jesus.
Only through prayer
Can mountains move.
Only in His time
Can answers be reached.
Then only by faith.
Hell? Yes, it's there.
Hell? No way for me!
Believe and receive
The Lord Jesus Christ.
Hallelujah!

HOLD HIS HAND

You've got to know
That Jesus never leaves you.
If you are lonely,
You probably left him
By moving away
Down the wrong path.
He will never leave you,
So do not let go,
Do not go your own way.
Hold the hand of Jesus,
Hold it tightly,
Every hour of every day.
That monster Satan
Waits for an opportunity
If you let go His hand.
Beware, he is clever,
And he'll want to keep you!
Don't let go!
Keep close to Jesus

Live His Way, not yours.
He is your lifeline
As long as you live.
Holding His hand,
It's a joyful privilege,
Heaven on earth!
Some might say
"It's real cool, it's wicked!"
And it is as they say!
There is one big rule—
You have to tell others
To do just the same.
And don't tell just one,
But make it your priority,
That there is nothing better
For everyone
Than to hold His hand.
Hallelujah!—

HEAVENLY LANGUAGE

Hallelujah—what does it mean?
Without a dictionary,
It means very simply to me
Unlimited praise!
Yes a thousand times.
An undiluted *Thank you*.
It's a word of happiness
Way above all else.
But there is a danger
Of using it blindly.
Use it when with the Lord,
Thanking the Lord.
Not as a habit
For ordinary events.
Hallelujah is precious,
It is heavenly language.
There is another word
Of heavenly language.
Again, in a simple way,
This word is *Amen*.
Amen to me
Is a simple thank you

To our Father, God.
Amen can mean
"I mean it."
Amen puts a seal
On the words of your prayer.
Even on a short,
One-sentence prayer.
It is allied to praise,
It shows sincerity.
It is heavenly language.
Hallelujah and Amen
Are treasured words
To be used every day
If you love Jesus.
Use them with feeling,
With gratefulness
And with dedication.
Not for secular use,
They are God's words
To be used for Him.
Speak that heavenly language
Hallelujah!

HOW TO PRAY

The disciples asked Jesus,
"How should we pray?"
And Jesus taught them
The Lord's Prayer,
The model prayer for all.
We call it "The Family Prayer."
So start with praise,
Then go and thank Him
For every blessing received.
Then ask for forgiveness
For thoughts and deeds
That were not right.
Then petitions—
Simply—the needs of others.
Those you know need prayer.
Countries without freedom,
Persecuted Christians.
For churches that are weak.
For your pastor,
And for all the folk you know.
There is no one
Who does not need prayer.
Especially pray
For the sick,
The lonely.

The needs of others,
There is no end.
For yourself,
Pray for faith.
Your need for direction,
Your need for more strength
To overcome weaknesses.
Your need to be contagious
In your daily life.
Ask the Lord to help you
Bring more to know Him.
And always be thankful.
Thankful for Him
Thankful for everything.
But then give Him space
In this time of prayer
To speak to you.
Prayer is two-way,
Let your mind be guided
And prayer will mean much.
Talk to Him—yes, indeed,
But listening is a must.
Enjoy your time of prayer!
Hallelujah!

IF . . .

If is a weak word
But it carries much truth.
If is a look-back word,
A word of wishing.
"If I had found Christ
Years before I did,"
Is a wishful meditation.
"If I had spoken
To the man on the bench,"
Smacks of spiritual failure.
The word is of things
That might have been.
We have to be positive.
We have to lead the way.
Timidity is the reason
For every *If*.
Abolish them!
One minute, though.

At times *If* can be positive.
"If we pray more."
That sounds positive.
"If we plan a revival."
Another one to use.
So *If* for the future
And none for the past
Is the way to go.
But the ones for the future,
Carry them out!
Theorizing is stupid,
Action is blessed.
Make sure any *If*
Leads to victory.
To harvesting souls,
To serving Jesus.
Hallelujah!

I LIVE IN HEAVEN

I live in heaven
Right now.
Heaven on earth.
When we were born
Eternal life began,
Praise the Lord!
I chose
To follow Christ.
I found assurance,
I found love,
I found comfort.
And I've been promised
A wonderful future.
Yes, I still have valleys.
Heaven on earth
Still has lows.
But the way through
Is always certain,

And I know
How to keep close
To Jesus.
I want to share
The heaven I have,
I want all to know Jesus.
No one can have
Heaven on earth
Without sharing with others.
If any Christian
Lacks this feeling
It's a sign to pray harder,
Of more to do,
To take you to the peak.
Get in gear
And rejoice as you land
In heaven on earth!
Hallelujah!

I'M NOT SO BAD

You're not the only one
To think
They are not so bad!
Think, though—
Bad things are bad.
Just as good things
Are always good.
Maybe you thought
That being a Christian
Allows a little leeway?
Those minor slips,
Those petty fibs,
Those little slurs—
They all come under
"Bad is bad."
You look at others
In your church.
You think that some
Are hypocrites.
Judge not!
For you are not perfect.

Jesus told us
That no one is perfect.
The church is for all,
Especially for sinners.
The church is for healing,
For striving for good.
The church is for you,
To iron out those faults.
Be sure not to be
In wolf's clothing!
We need to be humble
To realize we ourselves
Need an overhaul.
Admit those faults,
Come clean with the Lord.
Tell Him you'll start afresh.
You're well on the way
To being close to Jesus.
The good in you will win.
Hallelujah!

I'M TOO BAD!

Many have to face the facts,
They've lived lives
With blasphemy,
Immoral living,
Drink and drugs
And other evils.
You name it,
It has been done.
Some in their sober moments
Regret the evils done.
Some think
They are too bad to change.
They know their wrongs,
They see a dead end.
Everything is black.
It's up to us
To tell them
That they are wrong.
They can be saved,
They are not too bad.
Jesus waits
To hear them repent.

Real churches
Are ready for every sinner.
Real churches will strive
To change each life.
For each man or woman
Who truly wants to change,
The way is wide open.
The church will not dwell
On sins committed.
The message is of love.
Total love from God
For all who totally
Wish to start again.
Have them sincerely
Seek full forgiveness.
Jesus will bring to them
Their new life.
Truly born again.
Too bad? Of course not!
Turn around
Worship Jesus.
Hallelujah!

IT'S FUN!

When did you have real fun?
That is,
Really lived on a high?
Some really believe
Christians are dreary!
They've just met those
Who are uncommitted.
Have you seen a drink ad
"Coca-cola is the real thing"?
Change it!
"Christians are the real thing!"
There is nothing better
Than a total Christian.
Nothing can be compared
To those who love Jesus.
It's fun, real fun!
You have real friends,
Trustworthy and loyal.
A brand new life
Filled with adventure.
Friendships bring joy
And every day feels new.
Only those who accept Christ

Can tell you how much
Everything has changed.
Ask one to tell you,
It can be life changing.
Dreary? No way!
The key to a Christian
Is love,
Love for friends,
Love for you,
Love for your future,
That cannot be dreary!
If you're not convinced,
Ask how to talk to Jesus.
Then ask Jesus
To show His way to you.
Then go ahead,
Try your hardest
To take the Christian road.
The road is clear,
No obstacles ahead,
Jesus is waiting.
Hallelujah!

JESUS CALLING

Jesus is calling
To you and to me.
To the saved
And to the unsaved.
If you believe
That He is your Savior,
Why should He call to you?
He calls to ask you
To do more and more.
So many do not know
His love and His Way.
Yet without more effort
Many are lost forever.
Just think about them,
Pray and be led.
Urge others to do
Whatever they can do
Whenever they can.
To the unbelievers,

Tell them the facts.
How Jesus suffered
Unadulterated pain,
The torture of crucifixion.
To show His love for all
In every age.
To make people realize
That love is supreme.
That love is the password
For all to believe.
That the change in life
Into belief of God
Is through the love
Shown by Jesus.
Tell them these facts,
Pray for them
And pray for the harvest
That your faith will bring.
Hallelujah!

JESUS CARDS

I'm not very good
At witnessing.
I've read of many ways,
Then thought of others.
It's the start that is hard.
Even hints from books
Are not so good for me.
Now I think I've scored!
I'm making Jesus cards!
I have noticed that many
Give out business cards
To those with whom they talk.
It is an introduction
To a business talk.
My Jesus cards will have
On one side my name
And contact details.

On the other Jesus' name
And suitable words
Of invitation, of truth.
Every word must count.
Each day those cards
Will be blessed with prayer.
That the message will land,
That the card will open
The way to Jesus.
It will still be a challenge,
Facing those I've never met,
But God willing,
The Jesus cards
Will open the way
I have found so hard.
Hallelujah!

JESUS IS COMING

Jesus has told us
To be prepared
For the day He will return.
That His return
Will be without warning.
Suddenly Jesus will return.
It could be on any day,
Any month or year.
One thing is certain,
We must be ready now,
Prepared in every way.
Are we ready?
Are we cleansed?
Have we been greedy?
Have we been self-centred?
Have we witnessed
And followed Jesus every day?
So many questions
Because we have not lived
As if Jesus were coming soon.

We have to spring clean
Within ourselves.
Wake up our churches
And each member.
Sweep away the signs
That show idleness.
Wash away the stains
That show impurity.
Be ready right now!
Live right now
And every day
As if Jesus were coming.
For this we must know,
He is always aware
Of what we are doing.
So it is now we have to say,
"Welcome, dear Jesus,"
Because he lives.
He lives right now!
Hallelujah!

JESUS INSIDE

There is a bumper sticker
With just two simple words:
"Jesus Inside."
The driver boldly testifies
That Jesus is within himself.
He has to be sure on this.
He must never fail
In his way to live.
One false step could say,
"Hypocrite Inside,"
And this just must not happen!
His sign tells all
Jesus is alive.
Jesus is real.
Jesus is a fact.
There are many ways
For Christians to show
That Jesus is Lord.
But which ever way,
We must be totally sure
That we will not fail.

We have a mission,
To save souls
And our example
Is to be worth showing
As we follow Jesus.
You may not have the sign
"Jesus Inside,"
But echo those words
In the ways you serve.
As Martin Luther said,
"Christians are little Christs,"
A challenge we must take up.
Our daily chores may make
This standard tough.
And yet, to follow Jesus
Tough though it is,
Leads to victory for yourself
And for those you bring
To Jesus, our Savior.
Hallelujah!

KNEEOLOGY

When do you pray?
How many minutes?
Is it a cold prayer?
A tepid prayer?
Just a routine, a habit?
Or is it full of warmth,
Full of feeling?
Which comes first,
Yourself or others?
Are your prayers
Like a shopping list?
Or do you fill prayers
With praise,
With thanksgiving?
Finally, do you talk
Nonstop,
Or do you listen as well?
So many questions!
Questions to point the prayers
The right way to God.
You must not be shallow,
Be deep-rooted with love,
With faith,
With a grateful heart.

Start each day with prayer,
Your first appointment.
Pray in your travels,
When you shop,
When passing a church,
When passing people.
Just a few sentences
On what you observe,
Then listen for feelings
That come from the Lord.
This praying as you move
I call "Kneeology."
It's close to praying
Without ceasing.
You walk with God
And you talk with God,
He leads your thoughts,
Your day reflects your prayers.
It's total praying
For your total day.
Move into it,
Be blessed.
Hallelujah!

LAUGH WITH THE LORD

Are we too serious
As Christians?
Some think we are
Too stern,
Humourless,
Grumpy,
Judgemental,
Without fun
And unable to mix.
Is it our fault?
Probably, sometimes it is!
We with our churches
Sometimes
Are too wrapped up
With events within.
We fail to widen horizons.
We may get comfortable
Just as we are.
It is the task of churches
To look outward.
Smilingly outward!
We have good news
To tell all people.
Good news comes with a smile,
With happiness,

With joy.
Good news comes with love
And love brings cheer.
We need to help
The lonely,
The sick,
The elderly.
We need to show
To the young ones
That church is fun,
That Jesus loves each one.
Yes, real Christians
Are full of joy.
Being a Christian
Brings happiness,
New friends, new everything.
We are blessed,
We have Jesus
And we can laugh
With the joys we have
And the joys we shall have.
Join us, you will find
Happiness beyond measure.
Hallelujah!

LIP SERVICE

The only service many give
To Jesus
Is lip service.
Giving outward signs,
Public signs,
But actually doing nothing.
Being mostly idle.
Maybe a five-minute prayer
And nothing else.
Just lip service.
Half-hearted believers
Don't reach Jesus.
There are so many
Who seem to think
Small tokens are enough!
They fail in every way
To reach their Savior.
If every Christian
Were truly a Christian,
The world would change
Dramatically.
Churches would overflow.
What holds this back
Are the half-hearted,
The static members,

The many "do-littles."
Dedicated doers,
Doers of His Word,
Steeped in prayer,
Dedicated right through
Are what are needed.
Without any doubt
Miracles would be seen,
Jesus would rule.
The lip service
So loved by Satan
Would melt away.
There is a great need,
An urgent need
For every church
To strive to change
Lip service
Into service for God.
To stir all members
Into all the way
Servants of Jesus.
Sound the wake-up call,
Change their lives,
That they may change lives.
Hallelujah!

LITTLE SAMUEL AND YOU

The story of little Samuel
Can help each one of us,
If we are ones who pray,
And all should be so.
Too often we fail
When we talk and talk
To tell Jesus our ills
And all our worries.
And of the things we want.
We may make mention
Of friends,
Of those who are sick.
Perhaps about other lands,
Then the prayer ends.
Something is amiss.
Read the great story
Of the boy Samuel.
Three times he went to Eli.
"You did call me," he said.
Then Eli realized
That the Lord was speaking.
And Samuel?
He went back to bed,

He listened again,
And heard God speak.
That is what is amiss
In our daily prayers.
We talk and talk and talk,
And then close with Amen.
We give no thought,
We give no time,
We have no chance
For the Lord to reply.
To guide through thought,
To direct our way.
God's voice for sure
Will guide our thoughts.
Learn to pause,
To ask the Lord to guide,
And give some time
In silent meditation.
Have patience in silence,
And then know,
That your prayer is complete.
Hallelujah!

LONELINESS

Living alone
The days drifted by.
Getting up,
Having breakfast,
Wash up,
Tidy up.
Listen to the radio.
Go shopping.
Then I saw a poster
At the little chapel.
"Come in for coffee."
I ventured within
And was met with smiles.
Warmth in the welcome.
Friendship from all.
Friendship that grew
As the weeks went by.
Then an invitation
For a Sunday service.

The worship was good,
Out went my loneliness.
I felt a new life,
I found a new friend,
Jesus as my Savior.
There was fellowship,
Something not had before.
I knew of one thing,
That loneliness had gone,
Gone forever.
There is a need
To search out live-alones.
To show them Jesus
And happiness ahead.
We must share Jesus,
Pray that He will show us
Those who need His love.
Hallelujah!

LOOKING BACK

Looking back
On your life gone by
Is not always good.
We wish we had
Done this and that.
There can be regret
And regret is negative.
It can be different,
Look back
At positive events.
Be thankful
For good deeds done,
For good decisions made,
For recovery when ill,
For jobs well done
And so much more.
The recollection of your learning
And of success.
Of how you made friends
Who are still close by.

You realize that life
Has been full.
Full of good things.
So much done.
But there is a gap,
A yawning pit!
In all your thoughts
Of all actions done.
You missed out Jesus!
How He led you.
How kept you safe
Right through your life.
How Jesus made the difference
Year after year after year.
Looking back is good,
Nostalgia is interesting
When you include
All that Jesus did
Along those distant paths.
Hallelujah!

LOVE (1)

What is love?
True love?
Real love?
Forget and ignore crudities,
The secular sorcery.
Loves' pinnacle
Is found in Jesus.
And in God our Father.
Read again John 3:16.
Love to the extreme.
So much love,
Almost indescribable!
Love must live
In every life.
Visiting the lonely,
Going to the sick,
Spreading happiness.

Love with emotion,
Love without limit
To be shared with all.
It cannot be sold,
It is free,
It is given
With no strings.
It is a precious treasure
And it is yours
If you know Jesus.
You will be filled with joy,
You will pass it on,
You will share
Hope
And hallowed happiness.
Hallelujah!

LOVE (2)

The greatest of words
Is love,
A word often misused
By the secular world.
Go back to Paul's
Glorious words.
"Love is patient,
Love is kind,
Does not envy."
No boasting,
No pride,
No rudeness,
No greed,
And rarely anger.
No grudges,
And no evil.
What could be better?
Love rejoices in truth.
Then there was
Practical love.
The love God showed

By allowing Jesus
To be crucified.
Love supreme
With capital letters!
So piteous
Is the unbeliever
That ignores
God's love.
Ignores the love
That Paul shared.
It is for us
To show this love,
Regardless of unbelief.
God loves all,
No exceptions!
We are commanded
To be doers.
Please help us, lord,
We love You!
Hallelujah!

LOVE IN OVERALLS

How do you picture
Most Christians?
Are they all dressed
In Sunday clothes?
Good for Sundays
To dress for the Lord.
But what about
The weekdays?
No need to dress up,
But are we Christ-led
On days of no church?
If Jesus were here
As a person, I am sure
He would visit prisons,
Would shop for the disabled,
Do home repairs,
Help the elderly,
And so much more.
So what should we do?
Just as Jesus would do!
But are we doing this
Or just living our way?
Such tasks,
Especially for unbelievers

Can be a true witness
Of the love of Jesus.
The first steps
To change their lives.
Move around and search
For those in need of help,
Freely given in friendship
And you witness
In no uncertain way.
Be sure that while at work
You tell them of Jesus.
As time goes on,
Ask them to consider
Knowing how Jesus loves them.
With prayer and action
You will find
God will be with you
And He will be there
To change their lives.
With you and like friends
Your church will be known
As a church in overalls,
Fit for the kingdom.
Hallelujah!

MAYBE YOU ARE A NICODEMUS

Have you read
About Nicodemus,
The rich, young ruler?
He listened to Jesus.
He knew He was right.
He came and asked Jesus
What he should do.
The answer was plain.
Jesus said,
"Go sell everything,
Then follow Me."
Nicodemus was too rich,
He could not obey.
Sadly he walked away.
It is the same for us.
Whether rich or not.
We have things we prize,
Things we want to keep.
Our lives have habits

We also want to keep.
Being self-centred
Can be hard to give up.
Yet all are small things
Compared with all
That Jesus sacrificed.
It puts us to shame.
Pull up your socks!
Forget yourselves!
Picture Jesus Christ
As He hung on the cross.
Don't be a Nicodemus.
Show your commitment.
You will never forget
The decision you'll make!
Joy with Jesus,
This so much more
More than anything you've had
Hallelujah!

MEET AT MY HOUSE

I saw a large notice
As I passed a church.
"Meet at my house,
Meet me on Sunday."
That church knew
What most people ignore,
That Jesus wants everyone
To come to His house
Each Sunday.
For those who love Jesus,
Carry a card, an invitation,
To hand to strangers
In supermarkets
And other public places.
It can be a life changer,
The reminder for all
To meet at God's house.
Our church has empty pews.
This is the fault of all,

Church members, the pastor,
And all who attend.
All have failed to evangelize.
Evangelism must be done
By every Christian.
Not just once or twice,
But as a constant work.
If everyone did their best,
Pews would overflow each week.
Take the resolve to your church.
Base all on prayer,
Then move to evangelize
In any way you can.
Always be prepared
To be ready to ask
At any time those strangers
To meet at God's house.
Hallelujah!

MISSED CHANCES

We are sorry, Lord,
For the many times
We've missed a chance
To save a soul.
None of us can say
That every chance was taken.
Our lapses and slip-ups
Are far too often.
Because of our negligence,
Souls have been lost.
We pray for help.
Open our eyes,
Open our ears,
And open our minds.
Too much theorizing,
Too many church events
Can muffle and block
Our plans to witness.
We seem to have had
No time to fish.
The time had been wasted.
If we can help

To save one soul,
We rejoice!
But only one?
There are countless numbers
We have not touched.
It's almost as if
We turn our backs
On those who need
Our Savior Jesus.
It's as bad as ignoring
Someone drowning.
Without our dedication
Souls are destroyed.
Every person in the church
Is duty-bound to fish.
Don't miss on chances,
May we never rest
But always seek
For the ones who are lost,
Eager and ready every day.
Hallelujah!

MUSIC, MUSIC, MUSIC

Music is something
Most of us enjoy.
God made us unique,
So no wonder what we like
Differs in many cases.
Some enjoy
Old-fashioned boogie,
Some Dixieland jazz
From New Orleans.
The younger ones
Like what we think
Are tuneless numbers
With strange-sounding names.
While classical music
Plods steadily on
For many of any age.
The love of music
Is a gift from God.
The talents of musicians
Also come from God
Whether acknowledged or not.
For countless Christians
Handel's *Messiah*
And similar works

Warm and thrill,
For God's majesty is shown.
For the country lover,
The sound of birdsong
Is a sound from God,
Sounds from heaven.
In our church,
We sing our gospel songs.
We love to sing
"Amazing Grace,"
"The Old Rugged Cross,"
And so many more.
Thank you, Lord, for songs.
Thank you for sacred songs.
Thank you, Lord, for those
Who come to You through song.
May we continue
To sing our praises
For hearts so filled.
Music so enjoyable
And all the best all come
Through You.
Hallelujah!

MY MOUNTAIN MOVER

There are countless names
Given to our Savior,
To Jesus Christ.
He is our fortress,
Our Rock,
Our cornerstone,
Our Shepherd,
Our Redeemer,
And a hundred more.
My favorite,
My most sacred
Is my mountain mover.
To Jesus,
Nothing is impossible.
Sure, we need faith,
And also patience
And more abiding faith.
Then to be steeped
In prayer.
My Mountain Mover
Changed me from unbelieving

Into believing.
Since then, He has used me
To do impossible work!
He has saved my life
At least three times:
From poisonous snakes,
From bullets,
And from what seemed
To be a certain car crash.
He has given to me
A life full of service,
With joy and miracles.
He lifted me
From deep depression
Onto firm ground again.
My mountain mover
Is the greatest.
Thank you, Lord,
I'm with you all the way.
Hallelujah!

MY TESTIMONY

Every Christian has a story.
I grew up
A preacher's kid.
Too clever.
I believed all religions
Were equal!
I kept that belief
As I traveled to Malaysia
At the age of twenty.
I landed on the island of Penang
For my first job overseas.
All was strange.
The people, the climate,
Everything.
Perhaps because of this
I searched for something,
Something familiar.
And I found it,
A Methodist church.
I attended Wesley Church
Week by week.
The church was lively.
Full of active Christians.
I started to attend
The youth fellowship.
Almost every member
Came from
Buddhist or Hindu roots.
Some had to overcome
Fierce opposition from parents.
So many testified to all

Of changed lives and happiness.
These teenagers were special.
Something new to me.
To find that being Christian
Was such a treasure.
So important
They had to sacrifice
Their loyalties for Jesus.
It stirred me,
It made me realize
Christianity was unique.
It was the only way,
There was no other way.
I was converted.
From then onward,
My life has been filled
With the wish to serve.
So much has happened.
So many adventures
And the impossible
Changed to possible.
I thank those teenagers,
I thank the Lord.
Since that time of change
Nearly sixty years has past,
I rejoice that the thrill
Of following Jesus
Is still as strong
And always will be!
Hallelujah!

NEVER ALONE

Following Jesus
Is no bed of roses.
We all have
Plenty of downs.
Family troubles,
Illnesses,
Depressions,
Unemployment,
Bereavements,
And plenty more.
Whatever the problem,
Even at the lowest point,
You have a friend,
Your Savior Jesus.
Think what He went through,
Then compare your problems.
Yours are so much less!
Even so,
They will not go away,
They have to be borne.
But your tunnel
Holds His light.

The light that shows the way.
Never rely on yourself,
The Lord is much stronger.
Always learn to talk,
To talk with Jesus.
Even when you feel alone.
Be sure He is there!
Let His light shine,
Shine within you.
Shine
That others will know
That you are blessed
And able to share
The Light, the way
To His glory.
Believe utterly in Him
And the downs will seem less
And the mountaintops good.
Your life will be
As a brand new person,
Filled with your Savior.
Hallelujah!

NEW WITH GOD

Start with the old.
Your life may seem good.
You may have a job,
You enjoy entertainment,
Good food is normal.
There is time to read
And have nights out.
Hold on, though!
Think of the future.
Give it more thought.
Ever heard of eternal life?
Listen to me right now.
You are living in eternity.
You have no choice.
Except how you live.
The choice of heaven or hell.
How do you know which way?
You have to face facts.
Those who do not love Jesus—
The Son of God
Who was crucified for us—
Those who ignore Him
Simply, plainly,
Go to hell!
Those who right now

Want to change tracks,
Change their lifestyles
And learn about God
And about Jesus His Son
Will be welcome in
Christian fellowship.
The way to the kingdom,
The kingdom of God.
Changing tracks
Makes you a brand new person,
What we call "born again."
You will find new life,
New ways,
New friends,
Everything just about new!
A life on fire
With the wish to tell others,
To bring them to the joy
Of knowing Jesus.
Shed the old you,
Take up the challenge.
Follow Jesus
Become the new you!
Hallelujah!

NO GOD

My friends—
You tell me "No God"?
You ask me to reply!
Can man create a rainbow?
The wonderful sunsets?
Take a little baby,
Any baby.
It is unique,
It is miraculous.
Can man make these?
Look at the stars,
You cannot count them.
Who placed them
In the infinite sky?
Someone did,
And that was God,
The Creator.
Go to a hospital,
To the recovery room,
Any hospital.
See the dedicated care
Given by the nurses.
They show love and concern,
Who gave these emotions?

At night in city streets,
In the nightclub area
You will find street pastors,
Ordinary people who love God.
Did man make that love?
Real spiritual love?
Can it be man-made?
Of course not!
Simply, God is love.
God, our Creator,
He is everything for everyone.
Things don't just happen,
They come from God
And you had better believe,
Believing is the key
To the kingdom of heaven.
No God? Only fools say this.
It's the dead end road.
Think as I have said,
Be born again,
Act now, the call is urgent.
Come and follow Jesus.
Hallelujah!

NO TIME FOR GOD

"Can't you see
I've work to do!"
Paperwork at home,
A full-time job as well.
There is no time
To waste on platitudes
About God.
If there is one,
He gave only
Twenty-four hours in a day
And every hour is taken.
My answer came quickly,
"You said *if* there is a God,"
Then I continued that
It shows you do not
Reject God completely.
The man sighed,
He was unchanged.
I prayed silently to God.
Then I asked him for ten minutes.

Ten minutes to change his life.
I started off by telling him
How I found Jesus,
And how it changed my life.
I went on to tell him
That Jesus loves him
Regardless of his present ways.
How Jesus suffered death
To show the depth of love.
How love rules everything.
How life becomes joyous.
How life is everlasting
And eternal.
I asked him to pray with me,
Heads bowed,
And in peace
We knew His Presence.
God? Yes, and yes again!
Hallelujah!

NOAH'S ARK

Some Christians
In Hong Kong
Had a great dream.
They dreamt of starting
A Christian theme park.
The center would be called
The Noah's Ark.
It seemed impossible.
Yet over the years
It began to take shape.
Local Christian benefactors
Were found to give support.
The YMCA and Boys' Brigade
And other groups
Joined together to help.
Land was obtained
Red tape cut through,
And building commenced.
The Ark was built
To biblical measurements,
It was massive.
Gardens landscaped
And the beach below
Fit well to the scene.
The animals in pairs,
All were made.
A ramp came down
And animals were seen
To be coming onto land.
The dream became reality.

Massive elephants,
Tall giraffes,
Stately camels.
Beasts of all kinds.
They came down from deck one.
Deck two was something new.
It was the deck run
By The Boys' Brigade.
Facilities for seminars,
For churches to be organized
For leadership,
For planning new ventures.
Then on deck three,
Half is a hotel for trainees
And half a hotel
For visitors to the Ark.
Outside in the grounds,
Further equipment
To train young people.
God helps change
The impossible
To very possible.
Now thousands can visit,
Opportunities will come
To show the good news
Of Jesus Christ.
The way has been opened,
And the way will be used.
Praise God for His help!
Hallelujah!

NONSTOP THRILLS

So many think
The Bible boring.
They have never read it
Properly.
They grumble over
Long family trees
And detailed rituals.
They fail to treasure
So many gems within.
God's Word
Must be read with faith.
Be aware,
Miracles are real,
Do not dare disbelieve.
Get thrilled
At God's power.
Get thrilled
Over epic episodes.
Moses the superman,
David and Goliath.
Tales of Abraham,
Of David.
His ups and downs.
His great writings.
Then about Solomon
And a hundred more

Old Testament heroes.
And believe all that happened.
Then to the New Testament.
The Birth of Jesus.
His boyhood.
Tales of His life
And of His death.
His resurrection.
How hundreds saw Jesus
The risen Christ.
Stories of His disciples.
Then about Saul
Changed into Paul,
The Road to Damascus.
His travels,
His persecution,
His shipwreck,
His imprisonment,
And all his writings.
Boring? Impossible!
Open your eyes,
Read the greatest stories
Ever been told.
Jesus is alive,
The Bible tells you this.
Hallelujah!

NOT NOW, LATER

A friend of mine,
When invited
To follow Jesus, said,
"Not now, later."
He was enjoying life
Just as it was.
Yet he knew for certain
That the right way
Was with Jesus.
It was like
King Agrippa
In the New Testament.
After listening to Paul,
He said,
"I am almost persuaded
To become a Christian."
He understood
Yet failed to take the call.
In other words,
He chose the road to hell.
My friend will go that way

If he fails the call.
Too many put this off
And never returned
To accept Jesus.
For any who feel
The way is not urgent,
It can be shelved
And done later on,
Realize it is rare
To return and follow God.
Decisions have to be made
Without hesitation,
Without any delays.
It is truly a lifesaver,
Far too important
To put on file.
Come to Jesus right now,
This is your time.
You will never regret
The decision to act.
Hallelujah!

NOTHING LIKE IT

There is nothing like
Being a Christian.
Once there
You are never alone.
Whatever happens
You've got the Comforter,
The Holy Spirit.
You started
By accepting Jesus.
Now you've gone
So much further.
As you've traveled
Along His road,
You've had peace,
A better understanding,
And at times
You felt

Like you floated on air.
Some call it
Mountaintop feelings.
Even valleys were not so dark.
Challenges changed
To adventures.
Prayer time seemed more sacred.
Indeed, all things seem to be new.
If you've not known
Not felt like this,
Get back to your prayers,
Really pray
For the Holy Spirit to enter.
Believe in faith.
You'll be on your way.
Trust Him.
Hallelujah!

OBSTINATE LOVED ONES

Just about everyone
Has loved ones
Who do not know Jesus.
It is harder,
Even heartbreaking
That they will not listen.
They rebuff attempts,
They turn their backs.
They are obstinate.
Then we pray for them.
Sometimes every day
And for many years.
Let them know
That you pray each day.
Come what may,

You love them
And God loves them.
And your prayers will continue.
Be assured that God listens.
Be assured in His time
Your prayer will be answered.
His time, not our time.
Have faith,
Believe.
Keep on knocking,
Never give up.
Thank the Lord
For one day
He will answer.
Hallelujah!

OLD-AGE BLUES

You've served the Lord
For so many years.
You've done so much,
And now feel sad,
Full of blues.
Lack of strength,
Senior moments
Gathering in number.
Hearing not so good,
Sight failing.
You feel demoted.
The church fails
To use you anymore.
And you are tired,
Tired of doing nothing.
You must realize,
No Christian should be blue.
Right through the Bible
There is no retirement.
The word cannot be found

On any page.
See your pastor,
Tell him of your need,
The need to be used
To serve the Lord.
Maybe as a counselor
Or to lead a prayer team
Of elderly Jesus warriors
In prayer before each service,
Before church meetings.
Prayer is the most valuable
Of all God's work.
You will find new life,
New vibrant work
And rejoice
When prayers are blessed.
You'll have no blues—
You're far too busy!
Hallelujah!

OLYMPICS

The Olympic Games
Sets high standards.
Every country worldwide
Strives to be
The very best.
It brings together
Every nation.
Some are small and weak,
Others mighty and strong.
They all have a common bond,
Their love of sports and games.
And at the higher level,
True sportsmanship.
The Olympic flame
Burns brightly,
It never goes out,
A sign of eternal bonding.
As long as nations exist
It is the greatest
Of all known events.
Except for one,
The one that matters
Above all else,
The eternal flame

Of the Holy Spirit.
That flame has never died,
It never will,
Whatever lies ahead.
The Holy Spirit joins us all
Together in God's family.
There are no boundaries
Nation to nation.
No passport required.
Color and language
Make no difference
All who love Jesus
Are joined as one,
Welded together in love.
The weak and the strong,
The brave and the timid
Are joined together.
Church labels that once divided
Have gone forever.
All are one eternally.
The spirit of the Olympics
A hundredfold.
Praise the Lord!
Hallelujah!

OSCARS

In our secular world
Millions and millions
Worship human "Stars."
The pop singers,
Film and theater folk,
And strange-looking freaks.
The younger generation
Has many as idols.
There are a few
Who are with good talent,
And a few who know Christ,
A very few.
Mainly glitz and glamour
And tawdry fame
Are the center attraction.
Red carpets and awards
Give the teenagers joy
And the Devil rubs his hands.
We all know the story
Of David and Goliath.
David doing the impossible.
We Christians, just like David,
Are not dismayed.
Screaming mobs at Oscars
And similar secular scenes,
They come and go.
Something so much greater
Will come and stay.

Revival will come.
Countless Christians
Are working to the call
To bring revival,
To change the world.
Prayers are pouring out
To stir our failing leaders,
And God will listen.
There is an urgency,
There is a feeling
That action be the aim.
Action that will continue,
Action that will not stop
Until revival comes.
This is no prophesy,
The needs through prayer
Are in the hands of God,
His Will will be done.
The Lord will be the leader,
He will direct,
He will inspire
And He will guide each step.
He has taught us faith,
We are prepared.
Dear Lord,
In Your time, we are ready.
Hallelujah!

OUT OF STEP

When you follow Jesus
You are out of step,
You are no longer
Part of the crowd.
Some will avoid you,
Friends may be lost.
"You're different,"
They say.
"You've lost the plot."
Don't drink?
Don't smoke?
Don't swear?
They give up on you,
They leave you alone.
But this is a challenge.
Jesus mixed with sinners.
You must do the same.
Your built-in happiness,
Your visual confidence,
Your friendliness,

All count to show
Christians are special.
They are not dull,
They are not dumb.
They have targets,
And the targets are plain,
To tell and to share
Jesus as Lord.
That Jesus loves all
Who need new lives.
The way to heavenly eternity.
Make it clear to all
It's a one-way trip
One way that leads to God,
There is no other way.
Keep telling,
Keep trying,
The Lord is with you.
Hallelujah!

PATRICK'S PRAYER

Way back
In the fifth century
Patrick—Saint Patrick—
Showed the path to Christ.
In a wonderful way
He showed
Just how Christ-filled
Was his own life.
He said,
"Christ be with me,
And within me,
Beside me and to win me.
Christ beneath
And Christ above.
Christ in the quiet,
And in times of danger.
Christ in all who love me
And in all they say."
That surely is the meaning
Of "Christ-filled,"
The way that you and I

Should strive to be.
Back to the familiar—
Walking with Jesus
And talking with Him,
Living the life
That we should live.
Cast aside
Flotsam and jetsam;
Be really, truly immersed
In the Holy Spirit.
Never be reclusive,
Never stand upon a pedestal.
Be humble and loving,
Openly certain
That Jesus saves.
Be like Patrick,
Make that your aim.
And thank the Lord
For everything.
Hallelujah!

PASTORS NEED HELP

Your church leader,
Your pastor—
He or she is dedicated
To serve the Savior.
Some have to minister
To more than one church.
Whatever their task,
They need help,
Your help.
Their first help
Comes from God.
Then they need more:
Support from all members.
Be sure to tell your pastor
To use all within the church.
To take the task of paperwork.
To share in visitation.
Ask to have a "pastor's Sunday"

Completely run by members.
A Sunday when all
Show they want to help.
A lunch where talk
And suggestions flow well.
Prove that there is
A team always ready
To take the strain,
To be disciples,
To move the church forward
In every way possible.
May your pastor feel proud
That he has so much help,
And with that help
Be sure that God's work
Will thrive and succeed.
Hallelujah!

PEOPLE MATTER

So many people
Do not believe in God.
They cannot see Him,
They cannot hear Him,
They cannot feel Him.
Just like Doubting Thomas.
Then some say
That churches just make money.
Others that Christians
Are all hypocrites.
The rest do not think.
Yet all these people
Have lives to live.
Worries galore,
Futures uncertain.
Every one of them
Need God.
They need to be told of Him.
The hard-core humanists,

Mostly leave them alone.
All the rest
Are those to try to meet.
It makes more sense
To write a list
Of those you know.
Explain to them
That people matter,
That God loves each
By name.
Tell how Jesus suffered
To show His love,
Pure, unadulterated love.
Every person matters,
And Jesus waits right now.
Prayerfully seek a decision,
And follow your aim
Jesus is waiting.
Hallelujah!

PEW POTATOES

The preacher
Has worked so hard
As he prepares his sermon,
A sermon he prayed
Would stir the congregation.
One he prayed
Would have lasting effect.
So often his good folk
Had sat, had listened.
So often they thanked him
For his message,
Then went home
And failed to follow
What he had strived to teach.
The name of "pew potatoes"
Could well suit
All of his flock.
What to do?
What to say?
How can it be shown
That Jesus is alive?
He prayed and prayed.
He asked for faith,
For the Holy Spirit
To come to his aid.
To move, to stir
His pew potatoes.
The next Sunday,
He spoke as follows:
"Brothers and sisters,
I've been led

To shelve my sermon,
To tell you my thoughts
On pew potatoes."
He told them
How inaction was an illness,
How he thought
That all must change,
That even potatoes
Have eyes and roots!
Then he praised them
For loyalty
And for their love.
Then he went on
To say they must grow
Through the power
Of the Holy Spirit.
That in this way,
Large crops would grow,
That harvests would be real.
That through
The Holy Spirit
Pew potatoes would change
To wide awake, devoted
Disciples of Christ.
God-led,
Living and loving,
Vibrant and vital,
Ready to adventure.
And the Lord ruled.
The potatoes were *gone*.
Hallelujah!

PLAIN SAILING

Some people think
Christianity is complicated.
Too hard to understand.
Too hard to follow.
Often weaker beings
Are drawn to paganism.
Paganism with no rules.
Just doing
All you want to do.
To ignore completely
The Holy Bible.
To think of it
As unreal,
As ancient,
As best left alone.
All that is the easy way.
Seemingly, eternally easy.
Easy ways make life easy
Until trouble comes along.
For instance,
Ever feel lonely?
Where can you find
Caring friends,
Friends with love,
Those who can counsel?

Ever been depressed?
What will you do?
Is there a comforter?
Usually
No one will bother
When you need real help.
Turning your life
Another way,
The way to be close to God,
That is the way for you.
You'll find love,
You'll find care,
You'll find comfort.
And life will continue
Always with Jesus
And His wonderful love.
Go the easy way;
The Devil will rejoice.
Go God's way
And all of heaven
Will resound with joy.
Be with the Lord,
Seek real eternity:
You will be born again.
Hallelujah!

POLLUTION

There is much talk
About pollution these days.
To many it is very serious.
Man is destroying
The purity
Of the air
And of the sea
With toxins and gases
And so much more.
Pollution is worldwide.
In China and Japan,
Face masks are used.
Go up the skyscrapers
And look down.
A permanent mist
That all breathe in.
The beauty of nature
Shrouded forever
Unless there is cleansing
And clearing for all to breathe.
Spiritually, we are just as bad.
Especially in the West.
Supposedly the civilized West.
Literately demoralized.
Almost totally polluted.
Standards have dropped
To abysmal depths.
There are Christians
Willing to excuse

Blatant looseness
With feeble platitudes.
Only the power from God
Can sweep away
The dense immorality.
The humanist gloating
And widespread paganism.
In spite of all this,
Nothing is impossible.
God wants us to be warriors.
Battling the odds,
Showing that God is great.
Fighting the sin sickness,
The humanist disease.
To overcome
The wiles of the Devil.
To stir church leaders
To move together
In concerted efforts
To lead every church
Into victorious battle
And spread the gospel
To suffocate the evil
In every way
Right through God's world.
It can be done,
It will be done.
Hallelujah!

POWER, PASSION, PURPOSE

There are three positive Ps,
Power,
Passion,
Purpose.
You have them,
Use them.
Then miracles will happen.
Power comes from
The Holy Spirit.
Anything can happen,
Anything will happen.
Passion is essential.
How can there be results
Unless you overflow
With emotion and zeal?
With total enthusiasm.
That is real passion.
And then purpose.
What is your purpose?

Simply, it must be
Doing whatever
The Bible tells us to do.
Being doers of the Word.
Not our ideas,
God's ideas.
The purpose firmly grounded
Will bring that passion,
That power of the Holy Spirit
Which will dwell within you.
Just take care
That you are led by the Spirit,
And be sure not to lose the way.
Those three Ps
Will assuredly do wonders.
Armed with these weapons
The Lord will be with you,
Revival will be real!
Hallelujah!

PSALM GEM

So many psalms
Are priceless.
Indeed, no man,
Not even King David,
Could have produced
One single psalm
Without God's leading.
They are alive
For they come from God.
Look at Psalm 139.
Parts of it.
It goes—
He knows us completely,
He knows our thoughts,
What we will say.
It tells
Of divine answers
To our prayers.
Wherever we go
He is with us.
Even in darkness
He is our |light.
It tells of our creation,

How wonderfully
We are made.
Then David asks the Lord
To search him,
To cleanse him,
To know him
Through and through.
Such great prayers,
Such great words
And so much more,
Just in one psalm.
Thank you, Lord,
For all these words.
For your comfort,
For your nearness
And your friendship.
Your care
And your direction.
May we study and reflect
These glorious words
And give You praise.
Hallelujah!

PARACHUTING

Most of us
Have never seen
A parachute.
Parachutes have saved
Thousands of lives.
Think a little further back.
The men and the women
Who carefully fold
And carefully check
Each parachute.
One small mistake
Could mean death
When used in emergency.
Those who bail out
To save their lives
Depend completely
On those who packed
The parachute.
They bail out in faith,
They owe their lives
To unknown packers.
Bear this in mind.
Think of your own life.
The times of distress.
The times of deep trouble.
Of depression,

Of illness,
Of bereavement.
And each time you bailed out.
And safely landed.
Maybe scared,
Maybe injured,
But safe.
Who was behind these scenes?
You surely know.
It was Jesus your Lord.
Did you thank Him?
Do you still do so?
Going over
The times He saved you?
Did you get that fiery feeling,
The desire to serve Him?
Think on those dark valleys.
Live through them
And be very grateful
That Jesus was with you.
He has time and again
Rescued you.
His Love came through
At every point.
Never forget to be grateful.
Hallelujah!

PRAY-ER

You probably pray,
But not enough.
Prayer often starts each day.
One person said,
"It is surprising
What a non-praying church
Can do!"
True in some ways.
But with Jesus,
The mountain mover,
You will get miracles.
Start again with yourself,
At prayer.
You are the pray-er.
Think how great that is!
Somewhat like an ambassador
Meeting with his or her King!
You—the pray-er—
Talking with your King.
What a privilege!
What a great occasion!
If you think in this way
You'll not want to be brief
And go away
To get on with other things.
You'll want to take time
To worship,
To praise,
To show your thanks
And admit your mistakes.

And then with feeling
Express your needs,
Those petitions.
We must believe
That prayer
Is a royal occasion
And that a pray-er
Is a special person.
Do you see
Why the pray-er
And the prayer
are so important?
It should be so great,
And of course,
You will know,
You have to listen,
That when you talk
To your King
It's just not right
Just to talk and talk.
Realize He needs space
To talk to you.
Now you know,
Prayer is vital,
Be a warrior,
Be a true pray-er,
And this all through
Each day.
Hallelujah!

PRAYING PEWS

It is true
That before a service
Most worshippers pray.
Some for sixty seconds
And others much longer
With minds so full
Of weighted burdens.
In days gone by,
Most churches
Were enveloped in prayer.
Sadly, today many are not.
Many have no meetings
Just for prayer,
And those that do
Have few who attend.
That sort of church
Barely survives.
One thing is certain.
Prayer-conditioned churches
Will be or become
Pew-filled churches.
Prayer-anointed churches
Are filled with ferver.
For the prayerless church,
The days are numbered.
Praying pews
Need to happen.
It must happen
Or God is left out.
How can God lead a church
That never comes together
To really pray?
How can God lead you

And your church
If every member cannot see
That God is neglected?
Start that vibrant prayer meeting!
Prayers from the heart,
No holds barred.
Prayers filled with meaning,
Prayers you can feel
The presence of the Holy Spirit.
Pastors and leaders
Must be stirred in ferver.
So every church member
Knows full well
They must be part
Of God's will through prayer.
The breath of new life,
The reviving flame
Of the Holy Spirit for all.
Revive and revival,
Fresh and refresh,
Prayer must be the key
To unlock that door
To the overflowing
Of God's mighty power.
It is needed,
It is urgent,
Right now
And always.
Get to work,
Get to prayer,
Everyone!
Hallelujah!

PRAYER ON FIRE

I walked into a church
In Singapore.
A large church
With many people.
It seemed noisy,
Indeed irreverent
For just before a service.
I was wrong,
Very wrong!
All around the church,
In small clusters
All were praying.
Talking loudly,
Talking to God.
The screen at the altar
Had two words,
"Prayer Time";
It was a holy noise!
Prayer that could be felt.
The feeling of
The Holy Spirit.
It was a dedication
That God was present.
It pervaded every corner
Of that blessed church.
A few years later
That church had to move,

Move to a larger place.
The power of prayer
Showed proof
That where prayer is used,
Really used,
With utter faith,
Utter surety,
Utter ferver,
Miracles will come.
That same church
Goes from strength to strength.
More services are held,
More people pour in.
It is praying on fire.
Bringing powers unknown.
Prayer becomes so real.
At the end of a service
Many gather outside
To pray again
While others move in
For the next service.
And what are they doing,
Clustering in prayer.
Praying without ceasing
Is a great real way.
Hallelujah!

PROBABLY NO GOD

"Probably no God,"
Says an advert
On some British buses.
Proclaiming England's slide
Toward paganism.
Humanist propaganda.
But give it thought.
"Probably" could show uncertainty.
"Probably" can mean "maybe."
There is an element of doubt.
Poor humanists!
Anti-God people
Who show they want support.
Lonely people.
And their advert
Has opened the door
To Christian witness!
Their proclamation
Gives every Christian
An opening.
An opening
To talk on the buses.
About what is written
On each bus.
To tell travelers

Just how wrong
Is the advert.
It's a real icebreaker.
It gives us that opening
To tell of God's love
Even for humanists.
How He was crucified
To show His love
To every single person.
That there is no doubt,
He is alive,
He is real,
He is even in the bus.
The Lord was killed—
Yes, and rose from the dead.
Seen by hundreds.
Since then
Billions have found Him.
That love goes on and on,
It will never end.
Probably no God?
Feel sorry and help them.
God rules,
He always will.
Hallelujah!

QUENCH YOUR THIRST

Jesus talked
To the woman of Samaria.
About living water,
Living water.
The nectar
That all can enjoy
When we follow Jesus.
So many find it hard
To understand.
They are self-centered,
Self-satisfied.
Some are surface-satisfied.
Then, as with us all,
Troubles come.
Jobs may be lost,
Bills cannot be paid,
There are deaths,
There are quarrels,
Life has gone sour.
Darkness takes over.
The wiser ones
Begin to thirst,
Thirst for the first time.

Perhaps someone witnessed,
Perhaps they dusted their Bible.
Perhaps even read
Psalm 23.
Thoughts have been stirred,
The thirst gets greater,
And as God's way is shown
They learn to drink
Of the living water.
What of the others,
Those in darkness
Without that water?
They are the ones
We are called to meet,
To tell of the meaning
Of that living water.
We must pray to work
To show them His light,
And quench the thirst
For that life giving
Living water.
Hallelujah!

QUIET! LET GOD TALK!

Prayer is the key
To everything.
Nothing works properly
Without prayer.
Man-made plans are futile.
God-made plans are blessed.
Be aware
That prayer is talking to God.
It is the greatest
Of all tasks.
Talk and talk to God.
The more we do
The more it is blessed.
But give God a chance
A chance to talk to you,
A chance to lead,
A chance to direct,
To guide.
Be sure to meditate,

To pause
From time to time.
Pauses to feel His presence.
Pauses to have your thoughts
Moved in His direction.
Sacred silences.
It makes your prayer
So much more realistic.
Then pray again,
Then pause again.
You'll be soaked by the Spirit.
You'll come closer
To the Lord.
Then arise
And do
As the Spirit leads.
You've talked,
You've listened,
Now walk with the Lord.
Hallelujah!

READY FOR REVIVAL

Ready for Revival?
Yes and no.
There are the obstacles
That the Devil enjoys.
In many churches
There seems little desire
For real revival.
There is certainly
Lack of know-how.
So many non-doers,
So many retired
From serving Christ
Who do not wish
To be recalled to action.
Even pastors
Are sometimes in a rut.
Comfortable with their church
As it is.
Sounds gloomy,
But gloom can dissipate.

Jesus tells us,
"Where two or three
Are gathered in My name"
He is there.
So much can happen.
The power
Of the Holy Spirit
Can take over.
Contagion can start
With the two or three.
Prayer that glows
Can spread on fire,
Spirit filled prayer.
It can spread
Through the church,
The icebergs will melt.
Thank God for those
Two or three.
Hallelujah!

REAL FISH DON'T FRY

Eternal life is with us,
Right now.
The Lord has told us
To be fishers of folk.
Those who surrender
Fully to Him
Have that glorious promise
Of a move
To the heavenly land.
The land of peace
Free of sin,
No turmoil,
No friction,
Nothing but love.
It is God's land.
Eternally.
For those who choose
To go their own way,
The humanists,
The greedy,
The lustful,
The selfish,
And all who fail to listen,
It is quite clear,
They have eternity,
Eternity in hell.

Countless times
God's Word
Gives warnings,
And all have ignored.
But those who carry a sign,
The sign of the fish,
The sign of the cross
With all sincerity
Have full assurance.
They will be saved.
Those who are fished,
They are saved,
And the fishers
Are truly blessed.
Those that are fished,
They will not fry.
It is our bounden duty,
As Jesus commanded,
To be fishers,
To save those souls,
To give them
That great eternity.
Oh, Lord,
We thank You,
We praise You.
Hallelujah!

REAL RAINBOWS

Good old Noah,
Came through that flood.
And there was that rainbow,
A promise for the future.
Rainbows are good.
They remind us
Of that promise.
They echo God's greatness.
His wonderful creation
Is really real.
Rainbows bring cheer,
The end of a storm,
The end of dark clouds.
They signify
Calmness,
A respite,
A victory,
They are a special sign.
They are the same
As a light in a tunnel,
Showing better times ahead.
Rainbows lean to hope,
Bring relief,
Help give new life.
A rainbow is God's sign.
Thank you, Lord,
For rainbows.
Hallelujah!

RED ALERT!

It's no good
Pussy-footing about.
Unless your church
Is extraordinary,
It may be in great trouble.
On Sundays
Is it only half full?
Or even less?
This can be common.
How many days
Each week
Is your church
Filled with activity?
Tragically,
Most are shut most days.
Yet amazingly,
There seems to be no worry.
No red alert!
Nothing to stop the rot.
What has gone wrong?
Has the church given up?
All this need not be.
Our Savior
He is a mountain mover.
And yet the church
Has failed to use Him.

All has been negative,
No thoughts of the future.
There is no excuse
For any such church.
It is so plain, so simple.
Revive right now,
Or die when you die.
There has to be
A trumpet call.
Loud and clear.
A siren to sound
That red alert.
Revival means work,
Revival means prayer,
Revival means dedication,
And this will cause change.
Change into victory,
Change into God's will
And new life
In every toiler
Who brings revival.
Red alerts will work,
So promise your Lord
That your church
Will come to victory.
Hallelujah!

RED TAPE

As Christians
We are all supposed to be
Free of hate.
Perhaps it is the Devil
Who invented red tape,
And bureaucracy,
Rules with little reason.
Cotton wool padding.
Either from the Devil
Or just to test our patience,
Christ-led tests.
Sometimes red tape
Can be for protection,
Sometimes acceptable.
But when there is work,
The Lord's work,
Red tape can be an evil.
Even a secular trap.
Be positive,
Be practical.
Christ has no red tape.
The way to Him
Is direct.

There is just one rule,
Strongly so,
To love your neighbor
As you love yourself.
Love is the password
In everything you do.
Love is paramount,
But no red tape.
Love is sometimes hard
When someone has no love
For you.
Even so, cling to that love
That Jesus has taught,
Don't let go!
Never give up.
Jesus has never given up.
His love is supreme
So keep on His track,
The love track.
It brings you close
To Jesus Himself.
Hallelujah!

RESCUE SQUADS

Is it melodramatic
To have church rescue squads?
No way!
We have been told
To save souls.
Jesus told us
To be fishers of men,
Fishers of all.
But rescue squads?
Why not just
"Inviters"
Or
"Recruiters"?
Again—no way!
We are lifesavers,
Eternal lifesavers
And that eternally.
We are Devil fighters,
We are serious stuff.
Even our pastors
Rarely preach about the Devil,
Too scary!
But Jesus pulled no punches,
He made it clear,

Very clear
That the only two
Eternal places
Are heaven and hell.
Rescue squads are dedicated
The ultradedicated
To save those unbelievers
From that terrible hell.
How can we stand and watch
Friends and kin
Go down in hell?
How can we allow
Strangers to go to hell?
We must do
Whatever can be done.
Equipped through prayer,
Led by the Holy Spirit
To follow Christ's wish.
He loves each person
And so must we.
Do your utmost
And save those souls.
Hallelujah!

RETIRED

There comes a time
When we reach an age
That is called retirement.
The time when many
Regard as the time
To put the feet up
And to rest.
To call it a day.
This is so wrong.
You may well have served Christ
Faithfully,
Loyally in your working days.
Now you have far more time,
Time that belongs
To Jesus your Savior.
Turn to your Bible,
There is no place at all
That tells of retirement.
Read it and recall,
So many were serving God
In what we would call old age.
Abraham seemed to start
In his seventies.
Noah and Moses toiled for years,
As did many others.

Retirement is a challenge,
A challenge to start anew
With new way to serve God,
New ways and time to pray,
New ways to talk to others,
New ways to give support.
The way ahead
Is a way of adventure.
Age is your benefit,
Age means experience,
Age gives you insight
And so much more.
Never sit back
Except to plan!
And one other thing,
Prayer, it is said,
Is more important
Than anything else.
So much so it is
One of your ministries.
You've so much to do,
You're in your best years,
The years of retirement
To serve your Savior fully.
Hallelujah!

RETIREMENT BONANZA

Are you close to retirement,
The time most think of rest?
It's a great time.
But not so much the time
For all that rest.
Think on it.
Resting? Until when?
Until you die?
What a strange ambition.
Most who retire
Find that in one day
There are too few hours.
One man said,
"Lord, I need thirty hours
In every day you give."
There is so much to do.
Good things,
Helpful things,
Caring-full things.
You'll have plenty of plans,
Targets galore.
And for those who love Jesus,
So much service.

You've reached senior age,
But most likely
You still think in younger ways.
Time now to stir your church.
Make ripples that spread!
To lead
In prayer-conditioning.
To stir the need for extra witness.
Yes, even to lead
An A-Team!
To bring more to Jesus.
Many more.
It is great this retirement.
Each new day
A new adventure.
Full of joy,
Full of action.
Full of resolve.
The Lord does not rest
And neither will you.
Be joyful with the Lord!
Hallelujah!

REVIVAL WAY

For every church,
There are no exceptions,
There is an urgent need
To take the revival way.
Even churches
With pews that are full
Have to strive
To bring in more people.
The lost souls.
Most churches
Are stagnating or shrinking,
And yet seem blind
To their dire straits.
There is desperate need
For pastors
Filled with enthusiasm
To train and teach
All church members,
The young, the old,
To fish for souls.
Again, so sadly,

Few pastors have time,
Or maybe the inclination
To visualize the change
To a church overflowing.
The revival way
Is the only way.
It has to be so
For all Christ's churches.
Denominations don't count.
Fingers point again
To every leader
At every level.
Revival way is mandatory
To follow Christ.
It simply means we follow Jesus
To save lost souls from hell.
Lord, please help
To stir us all
To revival way.
Hallelujah!

SAVED? HOW, MAN?

Has anyone asked you,
"Are you saved?"
Did it scare you away?
The person who asked you
Had courage to speak
Even if his words
Seemed too direct.
There are better ways.
Maybe like these:
"Ever been to church?"
"What do think of God?"
"Ever met a Christian?"
Such questions
Make replies easier.
And can lead to
Good discussions.
The right idea
Is to open a gate,
To find a way

To bring the message
Of God's love
To those who never think
Of anything religious.
To tell how God
Forgives all sin.
That the door to God
Is open to those
Who so far
Reject His wonderful love.
Feel armed to talk
With openings
That do not scare.
And talk as friend to friend,
To introduce
Your greatest friend,
Jesus your Savior.
Hallelujah!

SECURITY MADNESS

For those who travel overseas
So much more is expected.
Extra photos,
Thumb prints,
Temperatures,
Eye checks,
Almost a physical biography.
Shoes examined,
Belts looked at.
Then no liquids allowed,
No scissors or penknives.
Allow for long lines.
They say it's all for safety.
Your welfare.
Then on the planes
Bendy plastic knives,
Same with spoons and forks.
All for your good.
Traveling with Jesus
Is far more simple.
Nothing needed as above.
Our Bible
Is our passport.
We travel with faith,
We travel with prayer

And our contact
Is Jesus.
We may be moving
Just around our town,
Or we may be called
To other lands.
But our main needs
Continue as our Bible
And our faith
And our prayer.
The man made security
Is something we may follow.
Until our destination
When once again
Our security is with God.
Heaven must smile
At man made hurdles.
The only hurdle to overcome
At God's great gates
Is the way in which
We traveled through life,
A pass or a fail,
And thank the Lord
And travel with faith.
Hallelujah!

SPECIAL

Special is a word
To use with care.
One way to use it
With freedom
Is for those
That love and serve
The Lord Jesus.
Real Christians,
Active Christians,
Fishing Christians,
They are the special ones.
The opposite
To pew sitters,
And the frozen chosen.
The special ones
Are the life of each church.
They can be contagious,
Hopefully to infect

The comfortable sleepers.
They can be of any age.
Children to very aged.
There are no age barriers
To God's specials.
None whatsoever.
The joy these people have
Can radiate
Way beyond the church.
For those not yet infected
It is not too late to change.
Change to being active.
To really enjoy
Closeness to Jesus.
As Paul has said,
"Become a brand new person."
Do that now.
Hallelujah!

SENIOR MOMENTS

If you are starting to age
You'll know all about
Senior moments!
You are introduced
To new friends.
And you forget the names.
You go to shop
And fail to buy
What you went out to buy.
You find it hard
To remember details
Of events last week.
Blanks that go on.
They can get you worried.
A daily diary does help,
Written memos,
A pocket notebook
And life is smoother.
There is always a positive side,
Sometimes overlooked.
Your spiritual memory
Is not affected!

Spiritually
You are wide awake!
You never will forget,
Jesus loves you,
That God is your Creator
And of your desire
To be steadfast in Him.
You still know how to serve
Your Lord.
You still can pray,
You still can thank Him
For every blessing.
You know you are close
To Jesus your friend.
Senior moments?
Yes they are there
But so is God
And that makes
All the difference.
Praise Him.
Hallelujah!

SIGNPOSTS

Have you ever thought
How valuable
Road signs are?
Take them away
And chaos will come.
Cities in gridlock.
We who follow Jesus
Have signs,
Directions,
For all our lives.
Whether we are young,
Or whether we are old.
Where are they?
In the Holy Bible.
Myriad signs.
On how to live,
How to believe,
How to love,
How to behave,
How to be moral,
Even how to lead,
And so much more.

Without our Bible,
With no gospels,
Our chaos
Would be insurmountable.
Signs are to help,
To educate,
To steer the way,
To show eternity.
Those who think
That the Bible is boring,
Dull and unreal,
Must be blind
To God's will.
They miss the great stories,
Challenges galore
And the signs
That point the way
To love and life.
We need those signs,
They show our way,
May we show others.
Hallelujah!

SIMPLY SIMPLE

So many like secular ways.
Nightclubs, bars,
Theaters,
Casinos,
Late night drinking,
Empty pockets,
Morning headaches.
So much and so little.
Much more remembered
Can be evening sunsets.
The morning sunrise,
The birds in song.
The dew-soaked grass
And scented flowers.
A walk along a lonely beach.
The colors of spring
And then of autumn.
God-given pleasures
From the Creator.
And all are free,

Freely given.
Those that spend
Their days so strangely,
Wasting their health
And all their wealth,
Their lives are dead,
Unless—unless—
Any we know like that
Are told of a better way,
God's way.
Pray for the Lord
To show you how
To change the lives
Of those who seem lost.
Try and clear the way,
Show the way
To the road
To Jesus.
Their lives depend on you!
Hallelujah!

SKYSCRAPERS

I've been fortunate.
I've seen the tallest
Of all skyscrapers.
The Empire State Building,
The Twin Towers
In Kuala Lumpur
And the Shanghai Towers.
Over a hundred floors.
And in Shanghai
Taller ones are being built.
No doubt others
Will strive
To be world beaters.
The aim
Is to go higher and higher.
That is a good example
Of what we should be doing.
We start by being born again.
Then receiving
The Holy Spirit.
We carry on
With help from the Lord.
We learn that whatever we do
There is more to do.
Trials, tribulations

Make us tougher.
We become able
To scale to heights
Not reached before.
Our life with Christ
Is a life of challenge.
Our aims must always be
To get higher and higher
In doing all we can
To bring others
To know of Jesus Christ.
Unlike the builders
Who aim for records,
Our aim is purely
In the service of the Lord.
Yes, we strive for the heights,
Of overflowing love.
Love that brings more
To know of their Lord.
Being on high,
A spiritual high
Is what all should attain
Help us Lord
To reach your heights.
Hallelujah!

SOUNDS TOO SIMPLE

You say
That Jesus will forgive
All that I have done
If only I believe.
It sounds too simple.
And it is simple.
But it is not a bargain,
There is no sales pitch.
God's message is simple.
You have to study carefully
The words of Christ.
Then within yourself
Know Jesus lives.
There is no litmus test,
Faith must be there.
Jesus knows your thoughts,
Your doubts.
He knows everything.
We are an open book
To Jesus.
It's no good bluffing.

Why is it
That Jesus forgives?
Because He loves you
And all who start afresh.
Simple, wonderful love,
Simple, wonderful forgiveness.
What you pay
Is simply to throw away
All sinful ways.
The dross in your life.
With help
To cleanse your thoughts
And all your ways.
You start a new page,
A clean page,
And with prayer,
With firm resolve
Each page will record
Great events in a new life.
Praise Him right now.
Hallelujah!

STOP WHINGEING

What does that mean?
It means stop moaning,
Stop being grumpy.
It's far too easy,
Even for Christians
To be grumpy,
To be negative.
We have to learn
To be positive people.
Dark valleys
Are commonplace,
But being positive
Brings you out
So much more quickly.
We must show
Cheerfulness as Christians.
Not artificially,
But because we are unbeaten.
Being loving
Brings resilient and
Then in turn thankfulness.
Positive thoughts about Jesus
Is better by far
Than long-faced moods.

If you feel down
Close the dark thoughts,
Come into the light
By listing your friends,
The good times you've enjoyed,
The good events to come,
And most of all
Your closeness
Your friendship with Jesus.
Grumpiness, whingeing,
Must be booted out.
Somersault into joy.
Swing into happiness.
Go and hug a friend.
And always remember,
Friends are with you to help.
Just as you are around
When they need help.
Friendship is the answer
Every time.
Did Jesus ever whinge?
Neither must you.
Hallelujah!

STREET PASTORS

What a challenge!
Some churches now train
Members to patrol city streets.
At night
Where there are clubs,
Bar and dance halls.
They wear a large sign,
"Street pastor."
Walking in twos,
Ready to help
Those who are sick
Or overcome by drink
Or even drugs.
They are not there to judge,
They are there
With Christian love.
They may be chastised
By revelors who hate
Those who love Christ.
Sometimes even struck.

But street pastors
Have come to stay.
Even the police
Respect them.
Why do they do this?
Because they do
Just what Jesus would do.
Jesus mixed with sinners,
He sat down with them,
He ate with them.
Street pastors are a living sign
Of a living Lord.
May they continue,
For this is God's work.
The church
At war with evil.
Striving to show
That love is above all.
Hallelujah!

TALENT TIME

The ordinary world
Loves to seek for talent.
New singers,
New dance acts,
Stars in the making
That will give fame
And fortune.
Generally of interest
But no intrinsic value.
Talents are fine.
God gave everyone talents.
Talents to nurse,
To write,
To teach,
To heal.
Talents to preach
And talents to care.
Others to counsel,
And those with music.
The list can go on,
And every one
Comes from God.
Go into your church.
Every member has talent.

Too often rusty or unused.
Hidden talents quite often.
They can counsel,
They can be readers,
They can be welcomers,
They can cook,
And they can witness.
Again, the list can go on,
And again all are from God.
The way to find
The sleeping talents
Is to enroll every member
In meetings.
Meeting to plan
Real ways forward.
Ways to bring people to Christ,
Ways to care for newcomers,
Ways to visit backsliders.
And use each person.
There will be great talents
Talents uncovered,
And your church will progress
To wonderful heights.
Hallelujah!

TEENAGER'S LAMENT

My parents are Christians,
They do not understand
Why I do not go to church.
The church is old,
And so are the members.
There are but a few.
Hymns are old,
And sermons boring.
What is the point?
If there were any youth,
If there were any programs,
There might be a chance
I would attend.
If I could meet
Any of my age
To tell me why they go,
I would listen.
My friends at school

Think that Christians are freaks.
Can anyone show they are wrong?
The church has no one
To talk to us,
No one to tell us
That God is real.
I've heard of city churches
That have many youth,
But there is nothing
In churches near here.
Seems to me
Members of churches
Just watch their churches shrink.
Are there no leaders,
Is there no one to really act?
Have leaders lost their faith?
There is no one;
There is nothing!

THE COMPOST HEAP

Good gardeners,
They all have
Compost piles.
Often started in autumn
With the fall of all the leaves.
Then are added weeds,
Dead flowers,
And other vegetation.
Kitchen scraps,
Shredded paper,
All go in to form a mulch.
Months later the pile has changed.
Out comes black soil,
The change from the rubbish
To good growing soil.
The way the compost goes
Is the way we seem to go.
We start as immature.
Gradually we learn of God.

As time goes on we change.
We change from being our own,
To being God's own.
As we learn to love
We become more rich.
We become more useful.
We grow, we mature.
The longer we live
The stronger we grow,
And mixing with those
Who do not believe
Can change them.
Thank you lord for helping us,
Helping us mature.
May we be the help
To change the unbeliever.
May our roots be firm
And our mission be strong.
Hallelujah!

THE CREATION

So much is said
About the creation.
But this I know
Completely.
For it is obvious
That the Lord God
Created everything
That lives,
That exists.
It is so utterly stupid
To deny creation.
Take an unbeliever
To sit outside
On a starry night.
Stare at the sky.
The countless stars
Twinkling in glory.
The planets
Glowing with light.
The moon softly lit.

Only God can create
That great universe.
Take the unbeliever
Into a garden.
Who can create such beauty?
Only God.
Go to a maternity ward,
Look at the babies,
All unique,
All created by God.
There is nothing that exists
Except through God.
Ugliness and evil
Come made by man.
Praise God for creation,
For the beauty,
For all good things.
Thank you, Lord,
For making me.
Hallelujah!

THE CROSS

The cross,
The most mighty sign
Throughout the world.
Bringing thoughts of Jesus.
When we pray
To picture His cross
Brings us so close,
Close to Jesus.
Thoughts.
On the utter cruelty,
Of the betrayal,
Pilate's mockery,
The sheer wickedness
Of religious leaders.
The crown of thorns,
The scourging
And carrying the cross.
The crucifixion,
Excruciating pain,
And below,
Mary and the disciples.
Such inhumanity
To God's own Son.
Why, oh why?
To show God's love,
To show His love
For all the world.
The biggest example of love

Ever shown.
These thoughts,
These pictures
Should be etched
On every mind.
For unbelievers
Who wear a cross
As a decoration,
We ask for forgiveness,
For they do not know
The meaning
For what they wear.
The cross shows us
Blood, grief, tears,
And then it shows love,
And ends with victory.
For Jesus is risen.
Jesus is alive.
May the cross
Stir us all,
Our leaders and ourselves,
To strive in every way
To serve our Lord
Who gave Himself for us.
We bow, we kneel,
Thank You, Lord.
Hallelujah!

THE GOOD SALVOS

Everyone loves
The Salvation Army.
They are welcome in pubs,
Allowed in clubs,
And accepted everywhere.
They are Jesus people,
And they are at work.
Whatever the trouble
The Salvos are there.
All through the world.
Earthquakes, fires,
Famine lands
And war-torn land
Quietly and seriously
Serving their Lord.
And in ordinary times,
At night in cities
They care for any
Who fall by the wayside.
No judging, just love,
Just the Jesus way.
A wondrous witness,
Sermons by action.
Radiating warmth,
Friendliness,
Going the second mile.
Thank you, Lord,
For your Salvos.
Hallelujah!

THE JACKPOT

So many people dream,
Dream of winning
A massive jackpot.
Probably a lottery.
Then dream of luxury,
World travel,
Big cars,
A big house,
Everything they want.
They have missed the truth.
Life is eternal,
Everlasting.
Our life on earth
Is just a passing phase.
They've ignored
The hereafter.
They've ignored
Jesus Christ.

They've ignored the fact
That Jesus died for them.
For those with sense,
With minds on track,
There is something
So much better
Than a million jackpots.
Eternal life with Jesus.
God's great kingdom.
A wondrous life
Beyond our understanding.
All we really know
Jesus will welcome us.
Jackpots?
No need.
We have Jesus.
Hallelujah!

THE LITTLE CHAPEL

In a village
Stands a little chapel.
Built by loving hands.
So long ago,
It throbbed with life,
Sunday school,
Prayer feasts,
A rustic choir.
And now?
A dozen saints
Keep the shrine from closing.
Each one treasuring
Good days gone by,
Loving memories.
What can be done
To save this godly house?
You have to begin
With far more prayer.
Doors are shut on weekdays.
Reopen for prayer.
Rock solid and regular.

Those prayers with pleas
For ways to revive.
And God will answer.
For faith that was dormant
Moves into action.
From static unbelief
Has grown emotion,
Emotion to hope
And hope to enthusiasm.
And ways will open.
New life will come.
Be sure, be certain,
And great is the future.
Those village chapels
Must never close.
They are sacred,
They are holy,
They will revive.
Believe and pray and do.
Hallelujah!

THERE IS NO GOD

There are times
When witnessing
That someone says,
"There is no God!"
So what do you say
To turn the tide?
There are many answers,
Try this one:
"So there is no God?
So you and I
And all our friends
Just happened?"
Then you can go on.
A wonderfully made baby
Just happened?
The earth,
The skies,
The stars,
The seas,
The hills,
And all else
Just happened?
All was just potluck?
That it was all magic?
Of course there is God.

Of course God created all.
Then go on.
Tell them
That historically
Jesus lived.
Jesus is a fact.
Ask your friend
If he thinks
That Jesus was a liar?
If he listens,
If he wavers,
Ask him about his doubts.
What is it
He cannot understand.
With God's help
You may well
Change your friend
Into knowing Jesus
As his Lord.
You've sown the seed,
You've helped him or her.
You've fished.
And God will take over.
Hallelujah!

THINK AND THANK

When you pray,
Do you take time
To think and thank?
Or are the prayers
A list of wants and needs?
Of future hopes,
Almost a shopping list.
How much time is spent
Just on personal needs?
How much for others?
Do we put ourselves first
Or last?
Where and when
Do we give our thanks?
Is prayer a selfish act
Or is it full of caring?
Try and change
The way you pray.
Begin with praise
And then to thanks.

Think of the things
That God has given.
Thank Him.
Your thank list
Is almost unending.
Then pray for forgiveness,
That list is long.
Go on to prayers
For others in need
One way or another.
Then at last
You come to your needs.
And God will listen.
Thinking and thanking
Your prayers are real.
Then add to them
During the day.
That's walking with Jesus
Hallelujah!

THINK HARD ON THIS

Do you like seeing
Empty pews?
Belonging to a
Shrinking church?
Does this have to be?
It does not.
Be inspired
With prayer and more prayer.
All of you,
Bring everyone
To the feet of the Lord.
Start with a week of prayer.
What is your cry?
For revival, of course.
The impossible made possible
In the only way,
By prayer.
Pray for your leaders
To lead in faith.
To believe upward

Is the only way.
Remember,
Jesus began
With twelve disciples.
Remember how Jesus told us
That He is present
Where two or three
Come together in His name.
You don't need vast numbers,
You need His Word
And you need real faith
And time unlimited.
You are His disciples,
You can,
You will change your church.
Fill the pews
And bring new life
Into your beloved church.
Hallelujah!

TRUTH DECAYED

Sadly, so sadly,
Some who loved Christ
Just drop away.
It might start
By forgetting to pray
Or missing the service.
The downward path
It never ends.
Like decayed teeth
Their truth becomes decayed.
The way to spiritual death.
Is there an answer?
Indeed, there is.
The comeback trail
Is the prayer trail.
Not sure what to say?
First, get a private place.
No noise,
No interference.
Then start with two words.
"Jesus, Jesus."
Stop and listen.
Repeat and listen.
No, there will be no voice
Booming out.
Your thoughts will shape

Into Jesus thoughts.
Maybe the cross,
Maybe His suffering.
Or maybe the peace
Of a babbling brook.
One way or another,
You'll be stilled,
You will enter
Holy ground.
From just those two words
You'll be led to more.
But always pause,
For the Lord to guide.
One thing for sure,
The prayer you do
Is the start of a comeback,
To return to your church.
You will know
You really missed Jesus.
Your upward path
Will be climbed in joy.
The truth that withered
Revived in full.
It's there to stay.
Hallelujah!

TSUNAMI

A word unknown
For many people.
Then came the big tsunami.
Waves sweeping inland
From Indonesia to India
And other far off lands.
Thousands were drowned,
Villages wiped out,
The power of nature
Was terrible.
There is another power,
Another force,
There is the spiritual tsunami.
The very first
Was at Pentecost
Through the Holy Spirit.
As years have gone by
There have been more.
John Wesley, with his preaching,
Was blessed with a tsunami,
The power of the Spirit.

In Wales a hundred years ago,
Thousands came to Christ.
Today in South Korea
A million find Christ,
The ripples extend
To Singapore and other lands.
It is time to pray
For a worldwide tsunami.
Nonstop prayer,
Every denomination,
Every member
And continuing.
God will listen
If all were to plead.
And continue to plead.
The whole Christian Church
Would catch on fire.
Wake up our churches,
Oh Lord!
Then bring us that tsunami.
We love you, Lord!
Hallelujah!

UP TO YOU

Each man and woman,
Boy and girl,
Live in his or her own kingdom.
It is a fact
That we are all self-centred.
Therefore each of us
Has to decide what we do
Today,
Tomorrow,
And every day.
We decide our own futures.
We hold our lives
In our own hands.
We may have had guidance
But many have not.
Because all are independent
There are barriers
That need breaking down,

Before we can
Introduce Jesus.
Barriers like brick walls.
It might seem impossible,
It would be
Without the Holy Spirit.
Each person
Who receives Jesus
Is a separate miracle.
That person
Has left the throne,
Given it to Jesus.
The kingdom
Now belongs to Jesus.
No more barriers,
Just love, wide open.
Hallelujah!

USE US

I've known the Jesus story
Since I was a little child.
I've been to Sunday school,
And then for years,
I've been to church.
My church is good.
There is fellowship,
There is much to enjoy.
Why are we so loyal?
What is the reason
That we love our church so much?
It is because we believe,
Believe in our Lord Jesus.
But something is missing!
Our numbers are static,
Even shrinking.
We've been looking inward
To each other.
We've failed to look outward.
Perhaps we lack a start-up.
Perhaps we are fearful
To talk about Jesus
To friends and neighbours.
It is so easy to tell them
About a new car,
Of new events.
The birth of a baby,
Some village news.

Yet when we need to tell
What Jesus means to us
Our tongues are tied.
We keep silent.
Oh Lord, please help us
Loosen our tongues,
Fill us with eagerness
To tell of a new life.
To tell people
That Jesus changes lives.
That real life begins with Jesus.
That they will be changed
As brand-new beings inside.
Then, Lord,
Our church will resound
As never before.
With real adventure,
Real excitement
And real purpose.
Real communion with You!
Please, Jesus,
Guide and direct us.
We want to follow You.
You are the needle,
We are the thread,
Use us.
Hallelujah!

WALKING AND TALKING

Walking and talking with Jesus.
You've heard this
Time and again.
Maybe sung it
To His glory.
But do you walk with Jesus?
Do you talk to Him?
Walking and talking
In this way
Will change your life.
Still have daily devotions,
Still read His Word.
Then, as you walk around
Or as you drive,
Talk with Jesus.
Passing a betting shop?
Pray for those within.
See some children,
Pray for them.
Passing a policeman,
Smile at him!
The same
With the garbage men.
And follow through
With prayer.
Every one of them
Have problems
Have worries.

And many do not know
That Jesus loves them.
Pray for them earnestly,
Even though
You'll never know
What answer
God has given.
Always remember
God loves all,
That the drunkard
Or drug addict
Is loved as much as you.
That every person,
Regardless,
Is to God
Important.
Pray without ceasing
Is the Brother Lawrence way,
Whatever you do
You do with Jesus.
Whatever you think
You think with Jesus
You live your day
Hand in hand
With Jesus.
Think His way,
Do His way.
Hallelujah!

WASHING FEET

Have you ever washed feet?
Someone else's?
Ever thought of this?
Jesus' love extended
To washing feet.
Are we too proud?
Do we shrink
From menial services?
It could be said
Washing feet is outdated.
Even so,
It would be good
To have an annual service
Just of washing feet,
To show each other
The love that Jesus taught.
That we may acknowledge
That nothing
Is unacceptable.
That love rules supreme.
Simple acts
Speak better than words.
Thank you, Jesus,
For showing what counts.
Hallelujah!

WE DON'T SELL GOD

Witnessing is not
Selling God.
We are not salespeople.
We have received
Our Lord Jesus Christ.
He suffered and died
To save us.
It cost Him so much
So we could freely receive
His love, eternal love.
We owe Him so much,
How could we sell Him?
You cannot sell love.
In many ways
It is hard to give freely
The love on offer.
There is resistance,
There is hostility,
Rudeness,
Ignorance,
Like a brick wall.

Even so,
We owe our lives
To Jesus Christ.
Brick walls,
Anything else
That is in the way,
Will be overcome.
We must plant the seeds.
Seeds we may not see grow.
But God will water them.
Witnessing is backed by Jesus.
Keep the faith.
Just one that is saved
Is something so great.
Saving a life eternally.
Not selling,
But telling.
And the Lord takes over.
Give Him the glory
Hallelujah!

WHAT IF

What if I did not have
Jesus as a friend?
What if life were empty,
Just meaningless?
No real life,
No real purpose,
No real love.
For the love
From Jesus
Is what brings us life.
Without the Lord Jesus,
Life would be blank,
Just nothing.
Just emptiness.
It's like a bad nightmare.
That "What if"
Does not exist.
We have Jesus right now.
We need never be alone.
Life is good,
It brims over with love,
With joy.
Life is so full
Because Jesus is here.
We are so glad,
We praise Him,
We worship Him,
We love Him.
Hallelujah!

WHERE TO PRAY

Where to pray?
May seem to some
A strange question.
We are told in the Bible
To be alone.
Not always easy.
The hustle and bustle
Seems to fill our lives.
The Lord will listen
Wherever you are,
But in the quiet
He seems close by.
If you have
A busy home
Insist on a period of quiet.
Susannah Wesley
Had many children.
Each day she signaled
For all to be quiet.
She threw her apron
Over her head
And peace prevailed!

.But prayer is for all time.
Learn to pray
As you walk outside.
Walk and talk
As you go along.
Pray on a treadmill,
Pray on a cycle,
Prayer is blessed
In a hundred ways.
There is no place
That prayer cannot be said.
Why not some special places?
Within a casino,
At a bar,
Inside a betting shop.
Places where prayer
Has never been said.
Invade the secular world,
Pour out your prayer,
God will be there!
Hallelujah!

WHEN GOD CALLS

Have you ever had
A call from God?
Did you feel
He had told you something?
To be a witness?
To serve the Lord
In some kind of way?
Maybe to start a project
Or lend a hand
To those in need.
Such calls,
Such urges,
Can change your life.
All come from God.
The greatest calls we know
Are in the Bible.
We read them many times.
But the calls we have,
Sometimes we brush aside.
We are busy,
We have our own plans.
And those plans
Are never as good
As God's plans.
The great call,
The great commission
In Matthew 28
Is a call to all of us.
Truthfully,
Honestly,
Have we done the same,
Brushed His call aside?

That call
Is so clear.
What have we done?
And what will we do?
Just think.
How many new faces
Are in your church?
None, or very few.
What have you done?
And other members
To answer Jesus' call?
Perhaps it is time
For your church to hold
A dedication service.
For all to pledge
To answer the call
To bring others
To know their Lord.
A dedication service
To bring to life
The church you love.
You read this now,
It may sound good,
But will you do this?
Bring your church
Into dedication
Just as described?
The call is with you,
May you be led
To stir your church.
Hallelujah!

WHO, ME?

It's been easy
To listen to sermons.
Some are interesting,
Full of stories.
Some tell us what to do.
Then by the end of the day
I've forgotten what they say.
Then one day
A new preacher.
With a resonant voice
And piercing eyes.
He preached
From Matthew 28.
"Go into all the world."
He seemed to point
His finger at me!
"Have you brought anyone
To Christ?" he asked.
I knew his message,

It was not new,
But this time it hit home.
I knew the Lord had spoken,
Spoken to me
I could not forget.
A message for me.
Yes, me.
No longer to be a watcher,
He called me,
To be a doer.
To move away
From being a listener.
Into the warmth
Of the Holy Spirit.
Praise God for that preacher,
Praise God for pushing me
Into the front line.
I love you, Lord!
Hallelujah!

WHOSE MONEY?

For dedicated Christians,
All money earned
Should be thought of
As from God.
And that a tithe
Should always be used
To His glory.
With regret,
Many of us
Do no such thing.
Some may serve the Lord
In many ways,
But cling
To all they earn.
There is so much need
To help the poor,
To give for missions,
To aid in many ways.
God gave us His Son,
He gave us everything.
This surely must show

What we should do.
And yet we fail
To give what is due.
Jesus saw the widow
With her tiny mite
And praised her.
She did far more
Than those with wealth.
She gave her all.
We must understand,
Giving ourselves to the Lord
Means giving all.
Pray about it,
Think about it.
Open your purses,
Your wallets
And do what is right.
And find that giving
Is a joy in itself.
Hallelujah!

WHY THE ONLY WAY?

A simple question
Simply answered.
In the Old Testament
The main message
Countless times
Is "Follow God."
In the New Testament,
Exactly the same.
Jesus tells you.
John the Baptist also.
Then by word and deed
So did the disciples.
So did Paul.
Then dozens of others.
Why the only way?
It is made so very clear.
There is just one way
To God's kingdom,
To eternal life with Him.
Oh, yes,
There is another kingdom,
Run by the Devil,

Eternal hell.
So terrible
That all with sense
Know completely
Of only one real way.
God gave us free choice.
The easy way
And His way.
Fools enjoy the easy way,
Self-centred.
Rejecting God.
Living life their way.
The way to hell.
Be sure,
Very sure,
You travel God's way.
The way
To the Promised Land.
Look forward to happiness
Eternally
And with your Lord.
Hallelujah!

WITNESS? NO!

Have you ever witnessed
About your Savior?
Most of us have not.
Most of us cannot.
We are tongue-tied!
What can we say
To break the ice?
Try these for starters:
"Do you ever go to church?"
Or
"Can I tell you
Why I go to church?"
Or
"Can you give me ten minutes?"
Oh dear, you say,
No, you say, not me.
Be sensible.
First a silent prayer.
Jesus listens,

He stands with you.
He will help you.
You can do it
Because of Him.
Don't be so negative,
Stop saying no.
Start with a friend
Who does not know Christ.
Give him or her
Your testimony.
And how it changed your life.
You planted the seed,
You did it!
Pray the Lord will water.
Finished?
No way!
Your adventure,
It's just started.
Hallelujah!

WORLD WONDERS

I've been privileged
To travel the world.
To see man-made wonders.
The Suez,
The Panama,
Crossing oceans
And seeing God's work
In many lands.
Man-made wonders,
Buildings, bridges, tunnels,
But always the greatest
Of things to see
Are those from God.
On the islands of Samoa,
All comes to a stop
Each Sunday.
For God.
Worshippers all in white,
All with Bibles.

In church no hymn books
All singing by heart.
No shops open,
No business,
Except with God.
In Singapore
Where churches outgrow
All buildings.
Infectious witnessing
In Asian countries.
So much to see,
So much to learn,
And all God-made.
If you ever travel,
Travel to see God,
Much more worthwhile.
And be filled with joy
From what you receive.
Hallelujah!

YOU ARE SO BORING!

I've heard it said,
"Oh dear, you are so boring!"
Even though I have enjoyed
All that happened today.
It is really hard to explain
To those who think
I'm dull and dreary.
There is so much to enjoy
Without watching
Bad language TV.
Without being hooked
Upon all the soaps.
So much to appreciate
In meeting with friends.
In reading good books,
In sports and games.
There is the treasure
Of Christian fellowship.
There is joy found
On Christian websites.
Then the thoughts
For plans and actions

In serving Jesus.
Even so,
Keep in touch
With the secular world.
Do not be ignorant
Of all around you.
Jesus always mixed
With every kind of person.
He did not isolate himself,
And he was never boring.
Boring?
That is so impossible.
Life overflows
When following Jesus.
Life is bursting with joy,
With hope and adventure.
Do your very best
To show to critics
That they are missing out
On sparkling life,
And tell them why!
Hallelujah!

YOU GOT A LIGHT?

Some Christians
Live as if in a trance!
Long faces,
Little to say,
Life in a rut,
No real joy,
No ideas to know the way
To a more joyful life.
They've lost the plot.
Before we go outside
To witness to unbelievers,
Turn toward
Those gloomy friends
Who have lost the plot.
Give them the light
That God gave you.
Be radiant,
Show that light.
Bring them to life.
Light within them
The glow of real prayer.
The warmth of friendship,
The eagerness of purpose.
Encourage them
To join you in actions.
Give them the light
That never goes out.
Then with your new friend
Look outward
And go and fish.
Hallelujah!

YOUR IDOLS

Believe it or not
Almost all Christians
Have idols.
Without realization.
How much time
Do you spend in prayer
Each day?
How much time
Reading the Bible?
How much time
In serving God
Each day?
Then write down
Time spent each day
Cleaning the car
Or
Gardening,
Or
Watching the TV,
And reading
Books and newspapers.
Or window shopping.
Then if you have a hobby,
How much time on that?

None of those are wrong,
But check on those
That take more time
Than time spent
With your Lord.
Are Godly ways
The losers?
Which have priorities?
Which are your idols?
It's an exercise
In putting God first.
Some though,
Can be changed.
Try prayer time in gardening.
As you garden,
Talk to the Lord.
The same with cleaning,
The same with traveling.
Bring God in.
Put Him first.
Just make sure
You have no real idols,
And then enjoy your day.
Hallelujah!

YOUR MOUNTAIN

Do you have a mountain?
Big problems,
Almost insurmountable?
There is only one way
To reach the top.
The way through God.
You see,
With Him,
Nothing is impossible.
With God as your guide,
There is nothing
You cannot scale.
We have to pray,
And keep on praying.
We have to have patience
And a listening ear.
There is no magic.
No instant wonders.
Mountain climbing,
Physically, spiritually

Takes stamina,
Takes persistence,
Hard work.
Spiritually include
Faith and action
And recognizing
God's way.
Problems are a challenge.
They toughen you,
And there is joy
When you reach the top.
Spiritual mountains
When taken to Jesus
Seem to shrink.
To hill size, Then to a hillock
And then to just a molehill.
Faith was the key,
Unlock that door!
Hallelujah!

YOUR PASTOR

About your pastor.
He or she is dedicated
To the Lord Jesus.
Pastors need your prayers
Every day.
Think of all they do.
Preaching,
Counseling,
Comforting, guiding, visiting,
And much, much more.
Then the mundane,
The paperwork.
Red tape from government,
Budgets for church.
Then funerals and weddings.
Pray for them.
Volunteer to help them.
Lighten their load
To give them more time
For spiritual needs.
Encourage more
To take on ministries.
Church teamwork
Brings strength
To your pastor
And to your church,
Your help makes a difference,
You're needed.
Go now and see your pastor.
Hallelujah!

YOUR RECORD

Give some thought
On what you have done
Over the years.
Write down the negatives.
Your weaknesses.
Be frank,
For the Lord knows all.
Little lies that were told,
Maybe a little cheating.
Times of envy,
Jealousy
And perhaps blasphemy.
Selfish acts,
Lustful thoughts,
Perhaps a little hate.
Yes, the Lord knows all.
Then from all you wrote,
Thank Him.
Thank Him
For wiping the slate clean.
For forgiving,
For giving us new life.
How wonderful that is.

Now be positive
On how you have changed.
Loving people,
Helping some,
Serving the Lord.
Witnessing,
Giving,
Caring,
Praising,
Worshipping.
Just being a Christian.
The Lord has said,
"No one is perfect
Except My Father in heaven"
This we realize,
So we do out best
To be near to perfect.
Always be close,
Close to Jesus.
His love is supreme,
Beyond all else,
Stay with Him.
Hallelujah!

YOUTH FOR CHRIST

We've all seen posters
"Youth for Christ."
Support this group.
Remember well,
Without youths
There is no future.
Without young people
The future is black.
And finally, dead churches.
Be realistic,
We have to find young people,
We cannot close our eyes.
It is said
That youth will not come.
Come to know their Savior.
We cannot give up,
It is not an option.
Some think committees
Are a waste of time.
Not this time.
Every church should aim

With top priority
To have a youth committee.
With a life of three months.
Then urgently plan
Events, publicity,
And regular dates for youth.
Ways that may be strange,
Ways that will attract,
Way that will work
To have the youth
Within your church.
Positive plans,
Feasible plans,
Purposeful plans.
God is with you,
He wants the youths,
With God, you'll win!
Be not dismayed,
Have faith,
There will be victory.
Hallelujah!

ZACCHEUS

Do you have
A favorite story
From the Bible?
I have one.
Look up Luke 19.
About Zaccheus,
The little man.
Unpopular with all.
A tax collector
Working for the Romans.
He wanted to see
Jesus,
Nobody noticed
As he climbed a tree,
A sycamore tree.
The multitude came,
There was a pause,
Jesus had stopped
At the sycamore tree.
Jesus looked up,
"Zaccheus," He said,
"Quick with you,
Come down."
The crowd was displeased.
Some of them booed.
This was the man
Who cheated them.
Who had greed.
Jesus ignored them.
He looked at Zaccheus,
He said,

"I am your guest today!"
Zaccheus was stunned.
Jesus smiled.
At Zaccheus' home
We do not know
All that was said.
One thing we know,
Zaccheus was changed,
Born again.
He said,
"I will repay
All whom I cheated,
Fourfold!"
So changed!
No more greedy grasping.
The meeting with Jesus
Turned right round.
Transformed,
By Jesus.
He had seen,
He had been called,
He had been saved.
This wondrous event
Can happen today
Jesus sees you,
He calls you,
Will you get down
And follow Him?
Will you respond
Right now?
Hallelujah!

5-STAR RACE

Have you ever run a marathon?
It's a five-star race!
It's tough,
It's for the toughest.
You need to train,
Maybe a whole year
To be ready for battle,
Come what may.
Just finishing,
Just passing the tape
Is a victory.
So it is to run the race
In your Christian life.
It's tough,
It's the toughest
And you need to train.
All the years of your life.
Stamina, lots of it.
Fit to serve Jesus.
Serve to the hilt.

You'll get tired,
May need first aid.
You'll need prayer.
This race is for all,
All who serve Jesus.
Half-hearted folk
Are disqualified.
Dormant folk,
Pew sitters,
With regret
Cannot finish.
You see,
Jesus died for us.
He sacrificed.
The supreme act.
Inactive Christians
Just cannot claim
They ever ran the race.
Be sure you breast that tape.
Hallelujah!

24/7

A weekly prayer meeting
Held in the church:
It was meaningful.
It was vibrant.
It led to greater aims,
And a prayer room
Was furnished,
Equipped with kneelers,
Tables and chairs,
Even a telephone.
Then books on prayer,
A prayer journal,
And a notice board
For any prayer updates.
It became the place
For twelve hours of prayer
Each day.
Public notices told all
To ring through for prayer.
It really was
What God had wanted.
As time progressed
More came to pray
Until the end target,
Twenty-four hours each day,
Every day.
A center of help,
Of care,
Of cheer.
A message
That Jesus loves all,

Regardless of whom.
All who call
Are treated with love
Through this prayer room.
For small churches
With only a few
Who can gather for prayer,
The same can be done.
Even just one hour a day
Is worth the effort,
For God is there.
Prayer is the key
To new life.
New visions, new life.
What may start
With just the hour
Can well grow and blossom.
Prayer brings miracles.
One day there will be more
To pray each day.
More hours in prayer,
More blessings received.
A lighthouse to all,
A beacon of witness
That never goes out.
That single hour
Of every day
Was the seed,
And the Lord
Brought it to fruition.
Hallelujah!

100 PERCENT

For every man,
Every woman and child,
For all who love the Lord,
There is a target.
Whatever your age,
Whether fit or disabled,
The aim is just the same:
To strive with every fiber
To be the ultimate Christian!
To be a Christian
As close as can be
To being perfect,
But knowing
Perfection cannot be.
Nevertheless, it is right
To aim for the top.

Without exceptions,
This is our aim:
To shine
As heavenly possible
In faith,
In service,
In going the second mile,
In sacrifice,
And in everything.
That is our aim
To the day
Of the clarion call,
When we are called
To the golden gates.
Praise the Lord!
Hallelujah!

TO WHOM IT MAY CONCERN

If I have inadvertently quoted directly from any book and not acknowledged anything, I am truly sorry and would acknowledge in the next printing if there has been such an error.

I do acknowledge being greatly affected by Bill Bright's wonderful book *Witness Without Fear*.

There are no direct quotes, but that book has greatly influenced me.

Dear Reader,
You've read the poems.
Maybe some you did not like!
Maybe some are helpful?
Maybe you feel God called?
Perhaps you'd like to comment?
On doubts,
What to do?
How?
Or other reasons.
You are welcome.
Godly fellowship should never close.
May God be with you.

pauljuby@gmail.com

Books of poems are books that are usually rarely read. This book is written out on a limb—a message of faith.

I am not a poet, but strangely, God led me to write more than one hundred fifty poems on one theme only—evangelism! Within the poems there are four main categories:

1. The unbelievers
2. The inactive Christians
3. The church leaders
4. Encouragement for active Christians

I am sure that we can do so much to bring unbelievers to know Jesus. I cannot understand why most churches are doing next to nothing to bring a revival.

The fault lies mainly with our church leaders who accept comfortable inactivity. Churches are shrinking and dying. There seems to be no major denomination on a red alert. Not one! Every denomination must be prepared to battle with Western paganism—not with pontifical proclamations from committees, but through vigorous and continual action.

This book, though, is a positive book. Every poem has a true *Hallelujah!* except for one, "Teenager's Lament." That poem portrays a tragedy.

Yes, this is a positive book because there are wonderfully positive Christians. And the few can change the whole scene with the help of God.

I thoroughly believe we can have revival—and in time even a tsunami revival—for God is in charge.

To any literary critics, enjoy yourselves! Poems by a non-poet I would presume would be way out of line. That is unimportant; it is the message in each poem that shines through.

I am praying and praying that some who read this will come to life, that some who have made no decision to follow Jesus will decide to do so, that there will be a contagion of enthusiasm. God bless every church that strives to bring people to the Lord! Amen.

P.S. It may seem to some that I am harsh when referring to church leaders. I am aware that they are good people. They are burdened with responsibility and overworked. But leaders have to lead. They have to break out of their traditional ways into being God-led, courageous, red alert leaders.